A FARM BOY GOES TO BIBLE COLLEGE

Steve Manley

Photos on cover:
    Kansas City College and Bible School

    Steve Manley behind the Pulpit of the Peoria Wesleyan
    Holiness Church

Copyright © 2012

by Evangelistic Faith Missions
P.O. Box 609
Bedford, IN 47421

ISBN 978-1-934447-48-2

Published by
Whispering Pines Publishing
Shoals, IN

Printed by
Country Pines Printing
Shoals, IN
USA

Dedication

"Who can find a virtuous woman? for her price is far above rubies" (Proverbs 31:10). Thanks to the leadership of the Holy Spirit, I attended Kansas City College and Bible School, and under the leadership of the Holy Spirit so did the woman who became my beloved wife, Helen Jean Denniston.

My pathway first crossed with Helen's in Overland Park, Kansas, during the Easter season in 1967. We dated as Bible school students, and eventually, I proposed to her on the Bible school campus. Both of us graduated from KCCBS. From there we went forth into the service of King Jesus.

Helen and I now have walked down life's pathway together for more than forty-three years. She has been my best supporter each mile of the way. Her love for Christ and her husband has meant

Helen and Steve Manley

more to me than I can express. She has been true to our wedding vows, "for better, for worse, for richer, for poorer, in sickness and in health." She has faithfully stood by me.

Helen obeyed I Timothy 5:14, "I will therefore that the younger women marry, bear children, guide the house, give none occasion to the adversary to speak reproachfully." She is the loving mother of our three children: Brenda, John, and Andrew. When the work of the Lord took me away from home for days at a time, Helen faithfully guided the home. The fact that our three children love and serve the Lord Jesus Christ is largely because of her steadfastness as a godly, stay-at-home mother.

As I type these lines, Helen is a loving grandmother to our ten grandchildren. Her home cooking, especially her cinnamon rolls, and those bags of Twizzlers strawberry licorice make her a favorite with all seven adventuresome grandsons and those three darling granddaughters.

I am a blessed man for having met, married, and walked down the winding course of life with my beloved Helen for these many years. It is a privilege to honor her with the dedication of *A Farm Boy Goes to Bible College*. Thank you, Helen, for all you have done for the Lord Jesus, our family, and me.

Contents

Foreword

It always is gratifying for our Kansas City College and Bible School alumni to represent the college well and make a mark in the world for God and His Kingdom. Steve and Helen Manley are two who have certainly been and are among that number.

Dr. Burl
McClanahan

Steve was a serious and sincere student who was determined to do God's will and respond to His call. It was always a joy to have him in a class, and it was an inspiration to see him grow and develop as a ministerial student.

Helen excelled in her classes, and after graduating she served the college as bookkeeper and secretary in the business office. I have not been privileged to work closely with them since they left KCCBS, but across the years it has been a source of encouragement to hear how God was and is using them in His church.

Many times as I have thought of Steve, I have recalled an incident connected with one of our college classes. The Lord gave me the privilege to teach a course in Foundations of Religious Education, and Steve was in one of those classes. During our study of Judaism, we made a field trip to an Orthodox Jewish Synagogue.

The rabbi welcomed us warmly, escorted us into the sanctuary, and asked us to be seated where the worshipers usually sit. He told us about their worship and showed us the sacred Torah, stressing its place in their worship and how it was cared for with great respect.

The synagogue was built so that the worshipers, as we were then seated, were facing Jerusalem. This was in response to King Solomon's prayer during the dedication of the temple in Jerusalem. He prayed: "If thy people… shall pray unto the LORD toward the city which thou hast chosen, and toward the house that I have built for thy name: Then hear thou in heaven their prayer and their supplication, and maintain their cause" (1 Kings 8:44-45).

The rabbi referred to the words of the Old Testament prophets concerning the coming of their Messiah. He made it clear that they still were expecting Him to come, and that was a central theme in their worship each Sabbath. I remember Steve's tender remark on our way back to the college campus. He said, "I wanted to give the rabbi a hug!" He was obviously touched by the fact that the rabbi was looking but yet had not found the Messiah. The compassion Steve showed toward the rabbi was an example of his love for all people, and, no doubt, has had a great influence in leading him to minister, not only at home, but also abroad.

I am glad that Steve has chosen to write his autobiography, and I am honored to share a few memories, along with a deep appreciation for students like Steve and Helen Manley. May God continue to bless them and use them for His glory until Jesus returns.

Dr. Burl McClanahan
KCCBS President Emeritus

Acknowledgments

In June 2011 the book *A Farm Boy from Fishhook* came off the press. I planned to write a second book *A Farm Boy Goes to Bible College*. Early in 2012 the Lord Jesus placed His thumb in my back and helped me to start the project. It was a little easier this time as I knew several of the steps that needed to be taken.

The book you hold in your hands was made possible by the faithful support of my darling wife, Helen. Without her painstaking proofreading and offering of multiple suggestions, this book would not have been printed. Thank you, Helen.

Ronald and Anna Smith have been extremely helpful in the development of this book. Their knowledge of preparing the book for publication has been a tremendous asset. May God abundantly bless them both.

It has been necessary to check with some classmates to be sure I had the details correct. Thank you Delbert Scott, Arlene McGhee, Gary Dougherty, Tom Peak, Kathy Sadler Anderson, and any other student who made deposits into my memory bank. Dr. Burl McClanahan also was a source of valuable information.

Story 1

A Sunny Day in August

The morning dawned clear and bright, and shortly after breakfast, August 28, 1967, I loaded my footlocker into the trunk of our
family car, a white 1962 Chevy Impala. My mother and brothers,
Rodney and Len, traveled with me to the Vernon "Tuffy" Dougherty
home on Front Street in Fishhook, Illinois.

Gary Dougherty was returning to Kansas City College and
Bible School (KCCBS) for his second year and was letting me ride
with him as I was planning to enroll as a freshman. When he saw
my gigantic footlocker, he laughed and said, "Steve, why don't you
put some wheels on it and just drive it to KCCBS?" I will admit that
the huge footlocker took up a lot of room in the trunk of Gary's
green 1960 Chevy Impala.

Jane Wardle was traveling with us. She was from the Terre
Haute, Indiana, area and needed a ride to Bible school, too. Jane
had lost her father in a mining accident, and big-hearted Gary
offered to take her with us. She had lived on the campus of KCCBS
the previous school year and had graduated from Overland Christian High School in the spring. Now she was returning to enroll as a
freshman in the college.

Soon the trunk of the Chevy was full. Then there were some
tearful good-byes, and Gary and I slid into the front seat and Jane
into the back seat. We headed for the "Y" west of Pittsfield and traveled west on Highway 54 to Kingdom City, Missouri, and I-70 west.
Not long after we got onto I-70, we stopped for dinner. I was to learn
later that the midday meal was called lunch, but to me that meal
was dinner.

By the time we arrived on the campus of KCCBS in Overland
Park, Kansas, it was rather hot outside, typical of late August
weather in Kansas. It was truly helpful to have Gary show me what
to do. He had lived in the boys' dorm the previous school year and
was acquainted with many things. Philip Estes, the acting boys'
monitor, allowed Gary to move into the room he had occupied the

previous school year. I selected a room across the hall from Gary on the second floor of the boys' dorm next to the monitor's apartment. Ruben Lowery, the boys' monitor, and his family had not arrived yet, and when they did, some changes were made, and Gary and I moved downstairs.

Boys' dorm on the campus of KCCBS

It was a new experience for a farm boy from Fishhook to live in a dormitory with many other fellows. I quickly got to know them as we introduced ourselves. We gave our names and stated what we were studying. Several of the dorm residents were ministerial students who came with the express purpose of studying for the ministry.

Not long after we arrived on the campus, Gary asked me if I wanted to go to the post office with him and two fellows who had arrived from Africa. I readily agreed and soon was introduced to Mesgun Tedla and Tekie Mebrahtu. Those men were from Eritrea, East Africa, and had been converted through the ministry of Evangelistic Faith Missions (EFM). I had never heard of EFM but soon realized those two men were fine Christians, and I was glad to meet

Tekie Mebrahtu and Mesgun Tedla

them. My introduction to EFM was rather unique as I met the product of the Mission before I ever met the director, Victor Glenn, or any of their missionaries.

It was different to be living in the city of Overland Park instead of on the Manley farm in northwestern Pike County, Illinois. In my heart I had the inward assurance that I was where God wanted me to be. It is wonderful to know that you are doing what God wants you to do and are living where God wants you to live. Psalm 4:8 says, "I will both lay me down in peace, and sleep: for thou, LORD, only makest me dwell in safety." It was so good to lay down in peace upon my bed in the boys' dorm. I was blessed in my soul, and I experienced great peace in obeying God even if I was in unfamiliar surroundings.

Story 2

Adjusting to College Life

The day after I arrived at KCCBS, freshmen testing for Bible and English placement was administered in the library. Many of us felt uncomfortable in our new environment but made the best of it. I passed the English test but was placed in the Introductory Bible class.

The next day we enrolled for our classes. I was asked what course of study I wanted to pursue. Frankly, I knew very little in what I should be enrolling, so the counselor suggested that because I had a call to preach, I should enroll in the Bachelor of Arts degree program and after that pursue a Bachelor of Theology degree. The classes in which I enrolled with the respective teachers included English Composition with Ida Belle Dothage, History of Civilization with Eli Crum, Physical Science with Dale Yocum, Introductory Bible with Ronald Hershburger, and Physical Education with David Newberry.

I was as nervous as a long-tailed cat in a room full of rocking chairs when I entered the classroom for the first time. However, I knew I was where God wanted me, and I was going to give it my best and trust the Lord to help me. I went to my room in the dorm after receiving the first assignments and read softly from my books. I was a poor reader, and by reading out loud it helped me to comprehend what I was reading and to avoid skipping the words that were not easy to pronounce. You see, I had become an expert at skipping difficult words. That caused much of what I read to make little sense. The professors gave each student a syllabus, and among other things it listed books that were to be read and term papers that were to be written. All of those things frightened the farm boy from Fishhook, yet he knew he was obeying the Lord, took courage, and pressed forward.

During the first chapel service of the school year, it was exciting to learn the names of the other students and from where they came. Gary Dougherty and I were proud to announce that we were both from Fishhook, Illinois. On one occasion in chapel, Gary jokingly said Fishhook was a suburb of Chicago. Actually, Fishhook is about three hundred miles from Chicago.

Eating meals on trays in the dining hall was far different than enjoying my mother's cooking around the family table where I could eat all I wanted. It was a major adjustment to have menus that were not like those that Mother selected. I made the best of it and learned to adjust.

My dear mother washed my clothes for me until I went to Bible school. When I left for school, she carefully explained what I needed to do to separate the clothes and prepare them for washing and with which ones I could use or not use bleach. She told me to take my shirts out of the dryer before they were completely dry and place them on hangers to avoid needing to iron them. Those instructions were written on a piece of paper and kept in my wallet for a long time.

A couple blocks from the Bible school there was a Laundromat where many of the students washed their clothes. Either on Friday evening or Saturday morning I made my way to "Clean-it" and cleaned it. If I went on Friday evening, I often was there when Martha Trotsky was doing the laundry for her and her husband, Paul. In 1995, I would visit them at Dot Lake, Alaska, where they were missionaries with EFM.

With rapid-fire adjustments, my head was sometimes in a spin. At the same time, the Lord was with me, and the inward assurance of being in the center of God's perfect will sustained me. The Apostle Paul says in Philippians 4:13, "I can do all things through Christ which strengtheneth me." Certainly, He strengthened me as I pursued my call to preach the gospel.

Story 3

My Family Came for a Visit

My parents and brothers came to visit me at KCCBS on Labor Day weekend. None of them had been to the college campus before that visit. They were excited about seeing the buildings and my room and looking around Overland Park, my newly adopted home.

Shortly after my family arrived, my father asked what I wanted to do. My response was, "Dad, take me out into the country. I want to see some cows, some corn, and some soybeans." Soon we were headed south on Metcalf Avenue, and beyond the Metcalf South Mall, I began to see what I longed to see—Black Angus cattle, corn, and soybeans. The corn was rapidly losing its green color; fall was in the air. It would have been nice to have had a car so I could venture out of the city, but I had sold my 1953 Packard to Clifford Phillips, and now I could not go and come freely. I was dependent upon others for transportation.

All too quickly Dad, Mom, Rodney, and Len were headed back to Fishhook and the Manley farm, and I was headed to my classes. Mother was faithful to write to me every week while I was in Bible school. I tried to return the favor by writing to her. Phone calls were expensive in those days, but my parents gave me a phone credit card and permitted me to call home free of charge. I tried not to abuse that luxury, but it surely was good to slip to the pay phone and check on the happenings around Fishhook. The news often consisted of the birth of a new calf or calves, neighbors being sick, someone getting caught for speeding, or someone having a baby. In the close-knit Fishhook community, we were all like family.

Dad worked in the maintenance department at Gardner Denver Company in Quincy, Illinois, where he did a lot of painting; he also cared for the family farm in Pike County. Mother was a busy housewife and was responsible for two growing sons. The whole family did not make many trips to the campus of KCCBS during the four years I was there. It was a long, four-and-a-half-hour drive from the Manley farm to the Bible school campus, and there just was not much time to spare for trips like that.

Although my parents did not come often to see me, I did go home to visit them. Gary loved to go back to Fishhook and visit his family and so did I. Whenever possible, when the school week was finished, we headed across the "Show Me State" (Missouri) to the "Land of Lincoln" (Illinois), and visited our families. I recall on one of those early visits when we crossed the Mississippi River at Louisiana, Missouri, we took deep breaths of the fresh Illinois air. We would arrive rather late Friday night, and it was hard to wait for morning to come when I could put on my old faded blue jeans again. You see, they did not permit students to wear blue jeans on the campus except for Physical Education or for work hours. Before I was ready, Sunday afternoon rolled around, and we prayed and cried together as a family before I headed back to the Bible school campus.

That first semester was difficult because I missed both my family and the farm, but inwardly I knew I was obeying the Lord, so I hung in there. I sincerely appreciated the wonderful support my family gave to me while I was in Bible school. A minister friend of mine shared his testimony that when he prepared to leave for Bible school, his mother said, "Son, you will never make it." It must have been extremely hard for that young man to wheel his luggage to the train station in a wheelbarrow and know that his mother did not think he would make it. If my mom ever doubted that I would make it, she did a good job of faking it because she was my best cheerleader. Her love, prayer support, and homemade cookies kept me going forward.

The Bible says in Ephesians 6:1-3: "Children, obey your parents in the Lord: for this is right. Honor thy father and mother; which is the first commandment with promise; That it may be well with thee, and thou mayest live long on the earth." After I left home and was in Bible school, I believe I loved my parents more and honored them more than when I lived at home.

Story 4

My Home Church During College

Shortly after school started, the students were required to select a home church to attend. Gary had been attending the Church of God (Holiness) Church on 27th Street in Kansas City, Kansas. Because Gary had been preaching the night when I got saved, I trusted his judgment and started attending the same church. The pastor of the church was Reverend Ronald Hershberger. I met him before when I visited KCCBS and heard him preach at the Fishhook youth church. He had graduated from the Bible school a few months before and was married that June.

The congregation was not large, but some of the students from the Bible school attended and rode the church bus from the Bible school to the church. That helped make it possible for me to attend because I did not have a car, and the church was across town.

Pastor Hershberger was a very zealous man. He stressed proclaiming the gospel and had regular street meetings, nursing-home services, and also developed an outreach program to the community through the Every Home Crusade. I loved the outreach fervor of Pastor Hershberger and became involved in it.

I also helped to teach the young people's Sunday school class. The church did not have a large building, so that class met on the church bus. We had some great times in our mobile classroom.

In those days all who wanted to be spiritual liked being called old-fashioned. It seemed to be a badge of honor to be known as such. Today, that church would perhaps be referred to as a very conservative church. Whatever the term given, the people who attended dressed plainly, testified freely, knelt to pray, were not afraid to say "Amen" out loud, loved to pray with seekers around the altar, stressed prayer and fasting, and loved to sing in the Spirit.

Because the church was not large, it had a homey atmosphere, and soon I got to know everyone who attended. "Holiness unto the Lord" was our watchword and song.

I am thankful for the selection I made for a home church. I did not know that when I selected the Church of God (Holiness) Church on 27th Street in the fall of 1967 that I would be worshiping with those people for four years, but I did. I thank God for a church you can call your home church. That is the church you support with your tithes and offerings, you give it your time and prayer support, and you can be depended upon to promote it. Hebrews 10:25 says, "Not forsaking the assembling of ourselves together, as the manner of some is; but exhorting one another: and so much the more, as ye see the day approaching."

Story 5

Funding My Education

During the summer of 1967, I had worked on the Dougherty hay crew. It was hard work, but the pay was good for the Fishhook area. Tuffy paid his employees two cents per bale, and on a long day it was possible to handle 1,000 bales and earn $20.00. That included picking up the bales in the field, placing them on his truck, then taking them and stacking them inside the barn. Some days we handled 500 to 750 bales per day which was not bad by 1967 wages in Pike County. I banked as much of my hay money as possible. I had sold my 1953 Packard for $65.00 to Clifford Phillips and stuffed that cash into my Liberty Bank account. Daisy, my Guernsey cow, had been sold for $150.00 and that money was in the bank, too. Just before I left for Bible school, I sold my flock of sheep for $300.00, and those dollars joined the rest. I was feeling rather rich when I arrived in Overland Park. In those days it was possible to carry a full 15-hour college load, live in the dorm, and eat in the dining hall all for $400.00 per semester.

I was preparing for the ministry and knew God was pleased with where I was and what I was doing. The Fishhook United Brethren Church gave Gary Dougherty and me each an offering for our school bills which we both sincerely appreciated. Although the money given by my United Brethren friends was helpful, it certainly did not cover my school bill. I was not taking a single math course that first semester, but I soon realized that if I kept taking money out of the bank to go to college, soon my bank account would be depleted. About that same time Carl Myers, the maintenance man, asked me about doing some custodial work around the Bible school. That would give me a $1.50 credit per hour on my school bill. I agreed and soon I was pushing brooms and swinging mops in the auditorium building now known as the Cowen Auditorium.

The business office was located in the front of that building, and I got to know Carlos Ross, the business manager; Anita, his wife; along with Lucile Dudley, their co-worker. I soon learned that

Anita did not care to be called Sister Ross. It reminded her of the Roman Catholic sisters, and she did not care for that association. Then I mentioned that I was not overly fond of being called "Stevie." That settled it! From that day forward until she went to be with the Lord, I always greeted her as Sister Ross, and she responded by calling me "Stevie." I looked forward to cleaning the building just to see Sister Ross.

About that time Helen Denniston, an attractive young lady from Michigan, asked me why I was not driving a school bus for Clark's Bus Service. I responded by saying, "I am not old enough to get a chauffeur's license." I did not turn 18 until October 11, 1967.

Moving potatoes to the kitchen

Carlos Ross, the business manger at KCCBS

It was good to work around the campus and slow the flow of money from my bank account. I was beginning to slip into adulthood with its many responsibilities, and God was helping me.

The cost of education has skyrocketed over the years, but I am indeed grateful for the privilege of working my way through college. It taught me to be responsible with both my time and money. I believe it caused me to place a greater value upon my education because I had to work for it. I heard of a fellow stu-

Anita Ross, the bookkeeper at KCCBS

dent who was called into the business office about his delinquent account. He told the business manager that he was going to take care of his school bill as soon as he took care of his obligations. The business manager made it very clear that his school bill was one of his obligations.

Saint Paul gave the believers at Thessalonica some important information about a strong work ethic in II Thessalonians 3:8-10: "Neither did we eat any man's bread for nought; but wrought with labour and travail night and day, that we might not be chargeable to any of you: Not because we have not power, but to make ourselves an ensample unto you to follow us. For even when we were with you, this we commanded you, that if any would not work, neither should he eat." I have always enjoyed eating, and I was taught by my parents to be responsible for paying my bills, so it seemed that working my way through Bible school would be my lot, and it proved to be the case.

Story 6

Monday Night Prayer Meetings

Early in the school year, I was made aware of the Monday night student prayer meetings at the campus church. Philip Estes was the student in charge of opening the session, reading some Scripture, and taking prayer requests. Those activities took only a few minutes, and then the group of students prayed with the women on the left side of the sanctuary and the men on the right.

I was a rather young Christian and had not been in that kind of a prayer meeting before coming to KCCBS. Sometimes I ran out of things about which to pray and would be the first student to leave the church. As my prayer list grew, I spent more time in the prayer meeting and left with the main body of praying students.

As the months rolled by, it became apparent that those who attended the Monday night prayer meetings were sincere followers of Christ. Some students worked second shift and could not attend the prayer meetings but were equally as spiritual.

Frequently after our time of prayer, there were testimonies given, which were refreshing and helpful to me. I began to take note of the spiritually minded young ladies on campus who attended those prayer meetings. I realized that if I fulfilled my call to preach, I needed a praying wife.

There are benefits in praying together. Jesus taught his disciples to pray, and they followed Him to the place of prayer. It must have been a blessed time to hear the Lord Jesus Christ pray. It probably was soul stirring to hear Peter pray and then to hear Jesus softly say, "Do it, dear Father. Do it."

Jesus said in Matthew 18:19-20: "Again I say unto you, That if two of you shall agree on earth as touching any thing that they shall ask, it shall be done for them of my Father which is in heaven. For where two or three are gathered together in my name, there am I in the midst of them."

Do you pray with others? Do you have prayer partners? The disciples prayed together and so should we.

Story 7

Opportunities for Christian Service

Although I was only a college freshman, I had a strong desire to serve the Lord and advance His kingdom. I joined the Christian Service Organization; the sponsor was Gene Chavez. During one of our early meetings, we were told of a fellow ministerial student who had lost his job, was having car trouble, and perhaps soon would have to drop out of school. We were asked to pray for the student and to give him an offering to help him. At the time I did not have a job other than an on-campus job, the proceeds from which were deducted from my school bill. I was not earning any cash. Nevertheless, my heart was touched by the sad story, and I gave $5.00 to help the needy student.

Marvelously, that student quickly landed a job, bought a brand-new Mustang, and continued as a student. I must admit that it hit me rather hard. I had given sacrificially to help a needy student. I did not have a car, let alone a brand-new one. I did not have a money-making job, but somehow that needy fellow soon had everything. God gave me the victory over the matter, and I realized that God knew my motive. Even though I may have given an offering to a cause that might have been less critical than I was led to believe, I would not stop giving. I would weigh the matter and give whatever God told me to give in the future. I was giving it as unto the Lord and not to man.

Reverend Onos Hood, pastor of the Church of God (Holiness) Church in Bluejacket, Oklahoma, asked for a group of students from KCCBS to come in early December for a weekend revival at his church. The Christian Service Organization sent Robert Myers and me as the preachers and some young ladies to sing that weekend. The Lord helped me to preach the night it was my turn. While preaching I mentioned that when I got saved Jesus gave me a new song of praise. I had loved Rock and Roll music and was a fan of the Beatles before I got saved. After the service an elderly man pumped my hand and told me that he knew about the new song in the soul,

Christian Service Organization

FIRST ROW: Richard Carrole, Gary Dougherty, Gene Chavez, Sponsor, Paul Pruett, David Churchill, SECOND ROW: Terry Lane, Ruth Hosier, Paula Arender, Ken Snyder, Kathy Sadler, Kendra Mosher, Cathy McDaniels, Linda Lane THIRD ROW: Karen Lenville, Ron Churchill, Marilyn Cook, Michel Masden, Connie Dickson, Sherry Willis, Eldon Manners, Ruby Barnett, Edwin Manners, Dawn Russell, Kay Swearengin, Melba McGehee FOURTH

ROW: Rachelle Masden, Elizabeth Masden, Marcene Herbert, Mesgun Tedla, Elbert McGehee, Judy Heer, Harold Blair, Leta Durkee, Sandy Smith, Shukry Braik, Steve Manley, Judy Lawson, Glenda Simpson, FIFTH ROW: Judy Bauer, Bassam Sabbagh, Hashem Sweis, Carolyn Addleslburger, Robert Myers, Don Gale, David Blythe, Wayne Skeen, Tom Peak, Sherry Morrison, Dan Cook, Wadie Khashadourian, Dorthy Martin

too. When Jesus saved him, he quit singing "She'll Be Coming 'Round the Mountain" and "Clementine." It was not easy to keep a straight face because those songs seemed almost like church hymns compared to the music from which I had been delivered.

Gene Chavez also introduced me to services in the Kansas City jail conducted by men from Rosedale Church of God (Holiness) Church. Bernard Chapman and Oscar Nelson were faithful to that Sunday evening ministry. I enjoyed sharing God's Word in that jail. One thing about those services—we certainly had a captive audience. Sometimes there was heckling, but no one could leave the service once it started.

If a man wants to be a carpenter, he works with tools and building supplies. If he wants to be a mechanic, he tinkers with vehicles as well as studies books about them. I sincerely appreciated being a member of the Christian Service Organization because it gave me hands-on ministry experience. The Bible says in II Timothy 2:15, "Study to shew thyself approved unto God, a workman that needeth not to be ashamed, rightly dividing the word of truth." Classroom study of the Scriptures is certainly important to the development of the minister's knowledge of the Word of God. On the other hand, Romans 1:15-16 says: "So, as much as in me is, I am ready to preach the gospel to you that are at Rome also. For I am not ashamed of the gospel of Christ: for it is the power of God unto salvation to every one that believeth; to the Jew first, and also to the Greek." The Apostle Paul said, "as much as in me is, I am ready to preach." There was something on fire on the inside that caused him to verbalize the good news of salvation. The Lord had put something in my soul when He saved me and called me to preach, and I wanted to share it every time the opportunity presented itself.

Story 8

The First Time I Spoke in Chapel

As a born-again Christian who had only been walking with Jesus a little over a year, I dearly loved going to chapel services three times a week. The songs were inspirational, and the sermons were instructive. The testimonies were refreshing, and I learned how the Lord was helping my fellow students.

I could not understand why some students thought chapel services were boring and why others deliberately tried to avoid being present. Because I had a call to preach, I tried to learn as much as I could from each of the speakers and profit from what they said and how they said it. In many ways I went to chapel to get as much as possible from each and every service.

One day Gene Chavez, sponsor of the Christian Service Organization, asked me to speak in chapel; for some reason it was on a rather short notice. I had made a promise to the Lord that if He opened a door for me to preach, I would do my best to walk through that door and trust Him to help me. Bear in mind, I was a first semester college freshman when asked to preach. I had only preached a few times other than for youth church services at Fishhook. I did not have a folder full of sermon notes from which to draw. I had never had a speech class in my life. I was taking Introductory Bible because my knowledge of the Bible was limited. At that time I did not even know what homiletics classes were. Later I learned that homiletics is the art of preaching or the study of preparing sermons.

I prayed and prepared as best I could and went to the chapel service with my knees knocking. Dr. C.E. Cowen was then the president of KCCBS, and he was the master of ceremonies. He introduced me, and I got up and preached a very short, pitiful sermon and sat down. Dr. Cowen redeemed the time and expanded on some points from the Scripture that I had used, and the benediction was given. Students were delighted that the service was short because chapel was just before lunch. The student body immediately headed across campus to the dining hall, except for a defeated preacher boy from Fishhook. I headed straight to my room. I wept over the pitiful job I had done preaching in the chapel service. It was humiliating to have stood before my fellow students and to have done such a poor job of preaching.

Finally, I gained the courage to open my door and sauntered down the hall. Soon I encountered Dewaine Snider who was giving Dr. Burl McClanahan a haircut in the boys' dorm. Dr. McClanahan is one of the most gracious of gracious men. He is the embodiment of kindness. He said, "Brother Steve, I appreciated the good spirit of your message this morning." He could not say it was a good sermon. That would have been a lie. He could not have said you had an excellent outline because I did not have an outline. He could not say it was a great exposition of the Word of God because that would not have been true. That dear man said something kind that helped a young preacher boy a great deal. "I appreciated the good spirit of your message." Those words may have kept me from dropping out of the ministry. If I cannot preach great sermons, perhaps I can preach with a great spirit, the Spirit of the Lord. Proverbs 18:14a says, "The spirit of a man will sustain his infirmity." Although the words spoken by Dr. McClanahan were uttered many decades ago, they encouraged me then and have helped me to strive to always preach with a good spirit

The Bible says in Zechariah 4:6, "Then he answered and spake unto me, saying, This is the word of the LORD unto Zerubbabel, saying, Not by might, nor by power, but by my spirit, saith the LORD of hosts." The Holy Spirit working through the preacher makes all the difference in preaching. It has been my desire since I started preaching the gospel to always exalt the Lord Jesus and preach in the Spirit. I do not want to be guilty of ever preaching with a bad spirit. After King David backslid, he prayed in Psalm 51:10, "Create in me a clean heart, O God; and renew a right spirit within me." David wanted to have the right kind of spirit. That has been and still is my desire.

Story 9

Battling Homesickness

To say I never battled homesickness would not be true. The transition from the family farm in western Illinois to life in the metropolitan Kansas City area was not an easy switch for a farm boy from Fishhook. I knew that God wanted me at KCCBS, but I was no superman, and at times I longed to be back on the farm, especially because I did not have a car even to visit the country.

One Sunday evening after eating supper in the dining hall, I was walking across the campus to the boys' dorm. Perhaps my head was down along with my spirits when suddenly I heard a cow bawling. I looked up and saw a cattle truck northbound on Metcalf Avenue. The cow doing the bawling was a Guernsey like the one I had raised years before and had for my 4-H project. She was on her way to the Kansas City Livestock Market and was not happy about leaving the farm. With a lump in my throat, I watched that cow in the truck until she was out of sight. In my heart I was saying, "*Bossy, I know what you are going through. I miss the farm, too, and I don't like the city either.*" I swallowed the lump in my throat, went to my room, and got ready for church.

Just because you are in the center of the Lord's will does not mean you will not face storms and battles. In Matthew 14:22 we read, "And straightway Jesus constrained his disciples to get into a ship, and to go before him unto the other side, while he sent the multitudes away." The command was clear: Get into the ship and go to the other side. However, Matthew 14:24 says, "But the ship was now in the midst of the sea, tossed with waves: for the wind was contrary." The disciples obeyed Jesus and left in the ship but soon found themselves in a serious storm.

Many people believe that if they are in God's will, they will sail on a sea of glass. That is not always the case. There is a clear example of this in Acts 27:13-14: "And when the south wind blew softly, supposing that they had obtained their purpose, loosing thence, they sailed close by Crete. But not long after there arose against it a tempestuous wind, called Euroclydon." Just because the south breeze is blowing does not mean necessarily that you are doing what God wants. On the other hand there are times when the followers of Jesus are certain they are doing the will of God, but they get into extremely stormy waters by clearly obeying the commands of the Lord Jesus Christ. At times during my freshman year, I battled homesickness, but I never packed my footlocker and turned my back on KCCBS. I knew God wanted me there even when the white caps were foaming.

Story 10

Home for the Weekend

Because I was without a car my first year in Bible school, I had to depend on Gary to take me back to Fishhook. Gary loved to go home, so I was able to hitch a ride with him on various occasions. I realized that trips to the farm created a few problems. It cut down on study time and laundry time. My love for my family and the country normally prevailed, and I would jump into Gary's 1960 Chevrolet, and we would buzz back to Fishhook.

On Saturday morning I put on an old pair of blue jeans and an old shirt and enjoyed life on the farm. If I could help with some tasks around the farm, using the Ford tractors or other equipment, that was just icing on the cake. It seemed like Saturdays flew by, and then Sunday mornings were filled with Sunday school and church. We soon finished Sunday dinner, and Gary and I headed back to KCCBS.

I was so happy when Thanksgiving break arrived and I headed back to Fishhook. My dad was harvesting the corn that I had

John Deere A and corn picker used to harvest corn on the Manley farm. Donnie Bentley and Len Manley on the tractor.

skipped school to plant back on May 10, 1967. The Lord had blessed the corn crop, and because I had planted it a little thicker than I should have, it was a bumper crop. Bob Kirgan was picking the corn for Dad that year, but I got to help shovel some of those golden ears into the corncrib.

During one of those early trips back to Fishhook, Gary said something that shocked me. He said, "Steve, you are going to notice that after you have been away to Bible school, when you come back home, you just don't fit like you used to fit." That was shocking news; I had always fit at home. As the year unfolded, I began to realize what he was saying. I was becoming more independent. My family was functioning without me being present. I was loved and still part of the family, but things were changing. Could it be that verse in Genesis 2:24 was right when it said, "Therefore shall a man leave his father and his mother, and shall cleave unto his wife: and they shall be one flesh." I was going to need to give that passage some serious consideration. Leave and cleave. Leave and cleave. Huh! I purposed to study that subject more carefully when I returned to the campus, especially the part about finding a wife to which to cleave.

Story 11

School Revival

The word revival means "the act of reviving; restoration from neglect or depression; religious awakening" (*Webster's Dictionary*). Having been saved on Palm Sunday night during a revival meeting in 1966, I have always associated revivals with conversions. When I think of revival meetings, I have flashbacks of sinners seeking God for salvation and new names being written in the Lamb's Book of Life. My mother, Mary Balzer Manley, was saved in a revival when I was a small child. I was present in the revival meeting when my father, Harry Manley, was saved one year after I was born again. Pastor Clifford Phillips had cottage prayer meetings to promote revivals.

Although I had been saved only about seventeen months when I went to Bible school, I was thrilled when I heard we were going to have a fall school revival with Reverend Raymond Pollard as the evangelist and Troy and Margaret Cook as the song evangelists. When my friend Tom Peak and I began talking about the school revival, we decided to have prayer in one of the classrooms after he got back from his afternoon bus run and pray until time for supper. For approximately thirty minutes we prayed in classroom C-3, and God helped us. We were aware that some of the high school students were not saved and needed the Lord. At times we wrote their names on the green chalkboard and joined our hearts in prayer for their salvation.

The Lord met with us during those revival services that were conducted during the morning in the chapel and in the evening at the campus church where Dr. Dale M. Yocum was the pastor. Souls repented and found the Lord Jesus Christ as their personal Savior.

One evening God came in a special way and there was much rejoicing. I recall Dr. Yocum walking around the sanctuary with his hands lifted heavenward praising the Lord, and tears were streaming down his face. I had never seen a doctor blessed before, but he certainly was a blessed man that night. Many of those on our prayer list sought and found grace around the altar. My confidence in united prayer for special needs was greatly strengthened.

The Bible says in Matthew 18:19, "Again I say unto you, That if two of you shall agree on earth as touching any thing that they shall ask, it shall be done for them of my Father which is in heaven." Tom and I learned an important lesson that fall in room C-3: united prayer results in answers to prayer. Many years have come and gone since we prayed together in the classroom. Tom was a pastor for a few years, and then he and his wife, Sherry, served as missionaries to Peru for over thirty years. Not every lesson was learned in the classroom when a professor was giving a lecture. Jesus taught Tom and me some blessed prayer lessons as we knelt at His feet. Thankfully, these many years later Tom and I are both active in the work of the Lord, and we both still believe in united prayer.

Story 12

The Miserable Mumps

It was always great to slip away from the Bible school campus and visit my parents for the weekend. Those weekends slipped by quickly, and soon I was back in the classroom listening to professors, doing my best to take notes and comprehend the material that was being shared. Someone once said, "A college lecture is that unique event where the material in the professor's notebook passes to the student's notebook without passing through the mind of either." I think that may have happened at least a few times during my college classes.

A few days after a pleasant weekend on the Manley farm, I received a phone call from my mother telling me that the mumps had visited my brothers. Since none of us boys had had the mumps, Mother warned me that I might soon be getting them. She had heard about a shot that was available to prevent mumps and suggested that I get it.

In bed with the mumps

Well, Manley boy number three, good old me, came down with the mumps. Unfortunately, I had carried little Jeff Lyon off the church bus and into his home the night before I came down with the mumps. I was seated next to Eva Hobson in English class the day I got the mumps. Both Jeff and Eva joined me a few days later having very swollen jaws.

I was quarantined in a room in the boys' dorm that had a private bathroom so I would not expose any more students. I was

35

indeed miserable. Thankfully, Gary had recovered years before from the mumps, so he became my care provider. He brought me meals from the dining hall and even did my laundry. Tom Peak also had had the mumps, and he paid me an occasional visit. Ralph Riley stopped in a time or two as well, but for the most part I was a campus leper. No one wanted to get the mumps, so I was avoided like a New Testament person with leprosy.

Gary brought me my assignments, and I worked on some of my lessons, but I was not feeling up to doing much studying. The room in which I was staying was near the mailroom, and I could hear the voices of happy students a few feet away from my bed, but I was alone nearly all the time. Thankfully, some of my dear friends back in Fishhook who heard about my plight sent me some get-well cards. It certainly was good to hear from my Aunt Cleo; Mary Emma Kurfman, my former Sunday school teacher; and several others. I read and re-read those cards and the letters they included. They certainly meant a lot to a lonely, sick farm boy stuck in a dorm room for several days.

The swelling finally went away, and the allotted recovery time had been reached. I could leave my "cell" and walk down the hallways of the dorm and walk across the campus to the dining hall. It sure was good to get outside again, but I did not realize how weak I had become by spending so much time in bed. It was a struggle to get back to my room. I was exhausted when I arrived and went right to bed. The next day I was feeling stronger and attended classes. Dr. Burl McClanahan expressed his condolences and was pleased to see me up and about. He let me know that he, too, had had the mumps and understood my situation very well.

The Lord Jesus said in Matthew 25:36b, "I was sick, and ye visited me." During those long days in that private room, I longed for visitors. Because of the fact that many of my fellow students had not had the mumps, they had a justifiable reason for not coming to visit me. Nevertheless, I learned a valuable lesson when I was sick; sick people appreciate being visited. I was not studying Pastoral Theology that semester, but I certainly learned something about visiting the sick that I have never forgotten. Years later it helped me to be a more caring pastor than I would have been had I never had the mumps during my freshman year in Bible school.

Story 13

Term Papers

Having grown up speaking the Manley version of Pike County English did not give me any extra brownie points using correct English. Because of my poor English skills, I made the foolish choice of not taking English during my senior year of high school. Consequently, I found myself greatly handicapped when I learned that several of my courses required that I prepare a term paper.

After reading about the particular subject I had chosen for the term paper, I started working at the task of writing the pages in long hand. To say this was anything short of being painful and difficult for a farm boy from Fishhook is an understatement of the highest order. I worked on the term papers during the Thanksgiving and Christmas breaks. Thankfully in those days the semester did not end until mid-January, and some term papers were not due until near the end of the semester.

Once I had struggled through writing the paper, then it had to be typed, double-spaced with proper footnotes, and all the standard English guidelines. I had taken high school typing but was not a good typist and certainly did not understand all the required guidelines for a term paper. Katherine Hobson worked in the campus mailroom, and for 25 cents per page, she would type term papers for students who desired her services. She knew what the professors required, and she was a skilled typist. I was willing to part with some hard-earned money in order to meet the requirements to pass the prescribed courses.

Katherine Hobson, typist for my term papers

By the grace of God, the oversight of the teaching staff, and Katherine Hobson's typing skills, I was able to submit the required term papers on time to fulfill the require-

37

ments of my first semester at KCCBS. Although it was not easy for me, I did my best to meet the requirements of each class. My grades were not outstanding, but I was able to make it successfully through my first semester.

Proverbs 6:6 says, "Go to the ant, thou sluggard; consider her ways, and be wise." I tried to do each task to the best of my ability, and God helped me. Later I heard the testimony of a stuttering preacher by the name of August Luelf. When he enrolled in Bible college, he stuttered greatly and had an extremely difficult time speaking. During his first semester he enrolled in speech class. One of the early assignments was to read a poem in class. He was assigned one that had many words in it that gave him great difficulty and caused him to stutter. After receiving the assignment, he went to his room, got down on his knees, and prayed. He said something like this: "Dear Lord, I thought you wanted me to preach the gospel, and I thought you wanted me to come here to prepare for the ministry, but, Jesus, I must have missed it. Just about every word in this poem is one that causes me to stutter. I guess I will have to pack my bags and go back home." About that time the Lord spoke to August and said, "I will help you, August, and all you will have to do is stutter just one word at a time." He took courage and went to his speech class and stuttered just one word at a time. That story was very inspirational to me. Although I did not stutter, I certainly needed the Lord to go with me to each class if I was to complete the prescribed course and eventually graduate.

Thankfully, the same Jesus who helped August stutter just one word at a time helped me to complete and pass one term paper at a time. Thanks be to Jesus.

Story 14

Second Semester

The adjustments of attending college were many, but the Lord Jesus helped me through each adjustment and the many challenges of leaving my family and the farm to study for the ministry. At last the term papers were all completed and submitted to the teachers for the first semester, and final exams were taken. The semester break had been enjoyed, and it was time to enroll for second semester. Procedures were more familiar because I had gone through the process once before. I enrolled in History of Civilization, English Composition, Anatomy and Physiology, Music in Evangelism, and took guitar lessons. Registration went smoothly, and I enrolled for fifteen credit hours.

A new development took place in January of 1968. Dr. and Mrs. Dale M. Yocum and their daughter Carmen left Overland Park and moved to South Korea so that Dr. Yocum could teach in the Jesus Korea Holiness Church Theological Seminary in Seoul. Omar Lee became the pastor of the Overland Park Church of God (Holiness) Church adjacent to the Bible school campus.

Dr. Yocum had been my Physical Science teacher the first semester. I loved his class and the way he brought creation and God into science. He made science interesting and enjoyable. Normally, he taught Biology second semester; however, he could not do that while living in South Korea. Joyce Hartman taught Anatomy and Physiology second semester as a substitute for Biology. I ended up taking the class and learned a great deal about the human body. I agreed with the Psalmist who wrote in Psalm 139:14, "I will praise thee; for I am fearfully and wonderfully made: marvelous are thy works; and that my soul knoweth right well."

Many times in the course of life we do not realize why certain things happen when they do or even why they do, but we can look back years later and thank God for His wonderful providence. Dr. Yocum went to South Korea and was a blessing to many precious Koreans. He returned to the United States and became the president of KCCBS. Through his influence some of the Koreans later came to KCCBS. Kim Yong Yun arrived on campus at the beginning of my senior year when he was fifty years of age. Sung Kyun Choi came to KCCBS for the 1971-1972 school year. Many years later I preached in South Korea in the churches where those men were pastors.

It is great to be guided by the Spirit of the Lord. Psalm 48:14 says, "For this God is our God for ever and ever: he will be our guide even unto death." As we follow God's guidance, it is thrilling to know that He desires to guide us all the way through life, even unto death.

Story 15

Extracurricular Activity

As second semester classes started and I became familiar with the subjects, I enrolled in an extracurricular activity known as dating. As a minister of the gospel, I realized I needed a spiritual wife. I began to take notice of the young ladies who attended the special Monday night student prayer meetings. Helen Denniston seldom missed. I also knew that it would be important for a minister's wife to be a good cook because she would be preparing meals for a minister on a daily basis. Helen helped in preparing some of the meals in the school dining hall. I also was looking for someone who was conservative in her lifestyle. I had not forgotten Helen telling how she had driven her Ford from Thanksgiving until Easter without adding gas.

The Monday night prayer meetings were in the campus church about one-half block from the girls' dorm. On January 29, 1968, I just happened to walk with Helen from the prayer meeting to the girls' dorm on my way back to the boys' dorm. The next Monday followed a similar pattern. I just happened to be walking up the sidewalk beside Helen, and we talked until we arrived at the girls' dorm. On February 7, Gary and I

New dating couple: Steve Manley and Helen Denniston

41

happened to be at Burger King after the Wednesday night prayer meeting, and Dolores Leichty and Helen were there, too. I asked Helen to sit with me the next day in the dining hall for lunch when dating couples could sit together, and she accepted. Gene Chavez used the occasion to announce a new couple on campus. Hands clapped and some heads turned as we officially became the new dating couple on campus.

Saturday, February 10, I said good-bye to Helen in the Bible school kitchen before leaving with Tony Hauck for Dixon, Missouri, where I was to preach on Sunday at "The Nail." Helen gave me some peanut butter cookies to take with me. On February 17 we had our first official social privilege. Because I did not have a car, Gary and Dolores and Helen and I double-dated. We attended a street meeting sponsored by the church we attended. After the street meeting we went to the International House of Pancakes for something to eat. On our dates we frequently went to street meetings, revival services, or the inner-city mission where I preached.

One night when we had a date, we went to the Kansas City inner-city mission. Because no one else was available, Helen led the singing and sang a special—all without accompaniment. I preached about Zacchaeus. My Pike County English showed up that night when I said, "Zacchaeus, clumb down from the sycamore tree." Helen laughed so hard I thought she might fall off her chair. The drunks in the service did not seem to notice. Helen quickly realized that if things progressed, and we were eventually to marry, she would have a lifelong task of tutoring me with the proper usage of English.

Gary and Dolores got engaged in February and started making plans for a June wedding. Helen and I were not ready to take that important step, but we dated, wrote notes, and learned how to see each other as much as possible and still keep within the school rules.

When Helen's birthday rolled around on March 29, she wanted to go for tacos at a Mexican restaurant. I agreed to the little lady's wishes although it was my first time to eat tacos. We did not have Mexican food in Pike County. After the meal we went to a revival meeting at the Church of God (Holiness) Church in Kansas City North and heard Larry Warren preach. I gave Helen a Bible for her birthday and read Ruth 1:16, "And Ruth said, Entreat me not to leave thee, or to return from following after thee: for whither thou goest, I will go; and where thou lodgest, I will lodge: thy people shall be my people, and thy God my God."

I must admit that certain Bible verses were becoming more meaningful to me such as Genesis 2:18, "And the LORD God said, It is not good that the man should be alone; I will make him an help meet for him." Genesis 2:24 says, "Therefore shall a man leave his father and his mother, and shall cleave unto his wife: and they shall be one flesh." I often pondered Proverbs 18:22, "Whoso findeth a wife findeth a good thing, and obtaineth favour of the LORD." One thing was certain, I wanted to find favor of the Lord, and just maybe someday Helen would become my wife.

Story 16

Jail Services

As my freshman year in college unfolded, more and more doors opened for me to preach the gospel. I had a burning desire to share the Word of God and seek to help people know the Lord Jesus Christ as their personal Savior. I was saved and wanted everyone else to be saved, too. If anyone asked me to preach anywhere, anytime, for any kind of a service, I accepted the invitation. I never said "No" to a preaching engagement that I possibly could fulfill.

I started preaching in jail services the first semester when I was made aware of that open door to evangelism. Reverend Bernard Chapman and Reverend Oscar Nelson, two men from the Rosedale Church of God (Holiness) Church, went every Sunday night and welcomed Bible school preacher boys to join them. The main reason that I took guitar lessons during the second semester was to help with the music. One night I led the song service and did so poorly that the inmates howled like dogs. It was awful. My music skills never developed, and I soon learned to ask others to lead the singing.

Another night while I was preaching, a drunken man walked back and forth behind the bars ranting and causing a disturbance during our service. I kept preaching and gave an altar call. A man came to the bars to pray, but the drunken man kept disturbing us. The man with whom we were praying jumped up from his knees and started hitting the drunkard in the face. We had to call the guards to break up the fight. Needless to say, our seeker did not get saved.

Gary was preaching one night in the jail, and John P. came forward to pray. Gary prayed with John, and he claimed to be saved. Gary was overjoyed with his new convert. He asked John if he had ever known the Lord before. John said, "Yes, but I went and backslid thirty-seven times." During the years I was in Bible school, I saw John P. behind bars many times. Later I heard he was struck by a car and killed. I hope John made his peace with God before he died.

We never knew what to expect during the jail services. One night when I was preaching, one of the inmates was very intoxicated. He went over to the jailhouse commode, perhaps six feet from where I was standing, and flushed it a few times. The noise did not keep me from preaching, but when he placed his hand in the water of the commode and started drinking from it, I brought the message to a quick close. That was too much for a farm boy from Fishhook to stomach.

I appreciated the privilege of sharing the Word of God in the Kansas City jail. I have no idea how many times I preached there or how many people with whom we prayed, but God's Word will not return unto Him void. II Timothy 4:2 says, "Preach the word; be instant in season, out of season; reprove, rebuke, exhort with all long-suffering and doctrine." By the grace of God I did my best to do just that. In II Timothy 4:5 we read, "But watch thou in all things, endure afflictions, do the work of an evangelist, make full proof of thy ministry." Preaching in the Kansas City jail certainly gave me many opportunities to preach evangelistic messages. It is my prayer that on the Judgment Day there will be souls who will testify to being saved by grace through those jail services.

Story 17

Driving a School Bus

When I enrolled in KCCBS, I was only seventeen and could not get a chauffeur's license until I turned eighteen in October. I worked on campus the first semester, but after I started the extracurricular activity of dating, I needed more cash. I applied at Clark's Bus Service in Merriam, Kansas, to drive a bus but had not heard anything from them, so I thought I might apply for a job at King's Food Host across the street from the Bible school. As I walked across the school parking lot to apply for the job, the Lord told me not to go. I turned around in the parking lot and went back to my room. The next day I got a call from Clark's and started driving on March 1, 1968.

Clark's Bus Service

Many of the young male students at KCCBS and some staff members drove school buses for Clark's Bus Service. Although the business operated about seventy buses, there were no female drivers in 1968. It was a perfect schedule for part-time work. The school dining hall opened at 6:30 a.m. A fellow could get a quick breakfast, carpool to the bus garage, get his bus, head to his route to pick up the students for the senior high school, and deliver them. Then he did the same for the junior high students. From the junior high school, the driver traveled to the campus of KCCBS, parked the bus, and was on time for his first class of the day. At the end of the school day, the driver returned to the senior high school and took the students home. Then he went to the junior high school and took those noisy kids home. After the completion of that run, the bus was driven to the bus garage and parked overnight, and the drivers carpooled back to the Bible school, arriving about thirty minutes before the evening meal. It was a perfect job because the school vacations were the same as the Bible school, so the drivers could go home for Thanksgiving, Christmas, and Easter.

A bus driver received $40.00 per week for driving that type of run. If he happened to have a car, he carpooled to the bus garage, driving once per week. If he did not have a car, he paid 20 cents per day or $1.00 per week for his rides. Gas was selling for about 25 cents per gallon at that time in the Kansas City area.

When I took my driver's test at Pittsfield, Illinois, in 1965, I was very nervous. After all, Pittsfield had one signal light at that time, and it was frightening to have to go through that intersection with my parents' car. Now, two years later, I was driving a sixty-six passenger bus through the second busiest intersection in the state of Kansas. Wow! What changes had come to the life of a farm boy from Fishhook.

I got used to driving the bus but had a few hair-raising experiences. One morning I was driving after a very heavy rainstorm. The street on which I was traveling with a busload of high school students had water across it. I drove through the water, and it was much deeper than I expected. When I went to stop at the first stop sign, my brakes were wet and would not work, and I went through the intersection. I rapidly pumped the brakes because the next stop was at a busy street. Thankfully the brakes dried, and I was able to stop the bus without difficulty.

One afternoon I got into my bus and headed to Shawnee Mission South High School to pick up my first load of students. On the way I was driving on a two-lane street, and a yellow Mustang was making a left turn. In the bright sunshine I did not see the turn signal until almost too late. I slammed on the brakes and avoided hitting the car. I looked in my rear-view mirror, and Gary was following me at a rapid rate of speed and had not expected me to stop in front of him. He hit the brakes and turned the steering wheel but was unable to miss my bus. He slammed into the right rear corner and twisted the frame on the GMC bus. The left front corner of his bus was damaged heavily. We learned later that both buses were totaled.

Delbert Scott, a fellow student who is now president of KCCBS, came by the two wrecked buses and with his 8-millimeter camera photographed two bus drivers from Fishhook beside their wrecked buses. The bus company brought us each a bus to drive to complete our runs. I was extremely nervous after the accident. Driving a busload of students was not really a good idea then. When I went to pull out at the first signal light after getting the junior high students, I pulled the gear shift into reverse because of a different shifting pattern and could have hit the car behind me. Thankfully, I did not. When Gary was called into the office to give his report of the accident, the owner of the company was not happy. However, we both kept our jobs.

Over the years I have driven school buses and church buses many thousands of miles. God has been very good to me and my passengers, and the mishaps have been few.

Proverbs 29:25b says, "Whoso putteth his trust in the LORD shall be safe." Proverbs 21:31b reads, "Safety is of the LORD." I believe God has answered the prayers for safety in travel many times for my family and me. He can do the same for you if you but ask. Psalm 121:8 states, "The LORD shall preserve thy going out and thy coming in from this time forth, and even for evermore."

Story 18

Open Doors to Preach the Gospel

The Lord opened many doors for me to preach the gospel in 1968. A group of students from KCCBS went to Fishhook for the weekend of January 19-21—Gary Dougherty, Eldon Manners, Dawn Russell, Ruth Hosier, Mickey Masden, and me. The Lord helped in those services in a special way.

A group of students from KCCBS preparing to go for a weekend meeting. Boys' dorm on left and music hall on right.

I occasionally preached in street meetings on Saturday nights and in the Kansas City jail on Sunday nights. I also preached at the Kansas City inner-city mission when the invitation came. Our local church had nursing-home services, and at times I was asked to preach there. When I returned to Fishhook for a visit, Pastor Clifford Phillips often asked me to go with him and preach at Fishhook, Baylis, and Woodland. Those churches had a rotation, and two churches had preaching services each Sunday morning.

Pastor Bill Winebrinner asked me to preach an Easter revival on April 7-14. I was delighted to preach that meeting because it was in the church where my father received the forgiveness of his sins and became a born-again believer in a revival one year before. My Aunt Cleo Whitaker was a faithful member of the congregation and prayed much for me during that meeting.

Gary Dougherty was taking a group of students to Flint, Michigan, for a meeting that same weekend. Helen Denniston was going along to be with her family for Easter. Gary made a stop by Fishhook on his way to Michigan, and I was at the Dougherty home after the revival service when he arrived. I got the surprise of my life when Helen popped out of Gary's car. After giving my parents a call, I borrowed Tuffy's car and took Helen to the Manley home for her first visit. It was about 10:00 p.m. when she met Dad, Mom, Rodney, and Len. Then all too quickly, about one short hour, she was back in Gary's car and making her way to Michigan.

God helped in the revival meeting with Pastor Winebrinner, and God's Word went forth. Sad to say, no one was converted, but the Holy Spirit was faithful to convict of sin, of righteousness, and of judgment.

I spoke in prayer meetings, youth meetings, and Sunday services—anywhere and everywhere the Lord opened the door. Jeremiah 1:5-7: "Before I formed thee in the belly I knew thee; and before thou camest forth out of the womb I sanctified thee, and I ordained thee a prophet unto the nations. Then said I, Ah, Lord GOD! behold, I cannot speak: for I am a child. But the LORD said unto me, Say not, I am a child: for thou shalt go to all that I shall send thee, and whatsoever I command thee thou shalt speak." Those words, "Thou shalt go to all that I shall send thee" have been very special to me over the years. Wherever God sends, I do my best to go. The Bible says in Revelation 3:8b, "I have set before thee an open door, and no man can shut it." God has opened many doors for me, and I have walked through them.

Story 19

Mushroom Hunting

The month of May means different things to various individuals, but to those who have hunted morel mushrooms in Pike County, it means it is time to head to the woods for the mushroom season. Many of us who have been raised there have hunted those sponge-like mushrooms ever since we could walk in the woods. When fried and placed on a plate with a couple eggs, it is almost like manna from heaven.

The Manley family had certain spots on our farm that we carefully watched each year in hopes of finding either gray or yellow morels to fill our bags. We loved to hunt and eat them.

While going to Bible school, I longed to leave the city and hunt mushrooms. Being without a car, I could not go to the country and hunt them. However, I did come up with a plan. Helen and I were dating; she had never gone hunting for mushrooms in her life, and she had a 1959 Ford Galaxie. We would visit my family on Mother's Day weekend and go mushroom hunting on the farm.

We left early Saturday morning on May 11, headed east to Fishhook, and went mushroom hunting in the afternoon. Helen found something she thought was a mushroom and asked me to confirm it. I had to laugh when I saw what she was indicating. She definitely was not a farm girl, but I loved her just the same. We did find some mushrooms that day. That was the first time Helen got to see the Manley farm in the daylight. The previous month she was at the house after dark and only for about an hour.

In the evening Helen and I went to Siloam Springs State Park and enjoyed a cookout with the Spring Valley Church congregation. It was a pleasure to introduce my girlfriend to the people at Spring Valley and to enjoy the food and fellowship.

Sunday morning Helen and I with my family worshipped at the Fishhook United Brethren Church where I was saved two years before. It was nice to be with my mother on Mother's Day. After a

Rodney, Jerry Dougherty, me, and Len with Jerry's motorbike on mushroom weekend

delicious noon meal, Helen and I traveled back to KCCBS in her Ford.

During our time of dating, Helen and I got to know each other and each other's family. We discovered that our family values were very similar. Family values are extremely important to those who hope to have a happy home.

When Abraham sent his servant on a mission to find a wife for his son Isaac, he made it very clear that he was to get a wife who had similar values. Genesis 24:37-38 says: "And my master made me swear, saying, Thou shalt not take a wife to my son of the daughters of the Canaanites, in whose land I dwell: But thou shalt go unto my father's house, and to my kindred, and take a wife unto my son." It is very important that those who are considering marriage have similar core biblical values and that their families share those values.

Story 20

Your Application Is Late

As the 1967-1968 school year was coming to an end, I hoped to find work in the Kansas City area for the summer. I applied for work at Roadway Trucking as a dock worker. I did not get hired, so I called Tuffy Dougherty, my former employer, to see if I could work on his hay crew for the summer. Tuffy said, "Steve, your application is late, but I think we can use you." I could stay with my parents and work on the Dougherty hay crew.

The Lord helped me to finish my freshman year with enough credits to enter the sophomore class in the fall. On May 29 Helen took Hashem Sweis, another student, and me to the Union Station to catch a train to West Quincy, Missouri. We rushed to get on the train with our luggage. It was very crowded, so for about an hour we stood until enough passengers disembarked for us to get a seat.

On May 31 my father went car shopping with me in Quincy. We found a 1962 Ford Fairlane at Steve Noser Chevrolet that was a very clean car. After negotiating, we finally settled on the price of $800.00, and I drove the white, four-door, V-8, standard-shift Ford home. I dedicated the car to be used for the glory of God, and it became my sanctified chariot. Sunday, June 2, I drove my Ford to Quincy and preached both times at the Church of God Church, commonly known as Independent Holiness People, at 21st and Payson Avenue. Pastor Ralph Smith had a death in his family and needed someone to fill the pulpit. The first Sunday I had the Ford, I used it to go to a preaching engagement.

I was on the board of Whispering Oaks Youth Camp near Quincy and went to a board meeting on June 4. During that meeting I was asked to promote the youth camp by visiting churches. I was delighted to do so and booked a service at the Ft. Madison, Iowa, church where Leo Hanks was pastoring. Jerry Dougherty went with me for the service. I also booked a service at the church in Baden, Missouri, a suburb of St. Louis. Gail Griffith, Shirley Womach, and Judy and Jerry Dougherty went with me. Gail, Judy, and Jerry sang; Shirley played the piano; and I spoke about the youth camp.

Working in the hayfields was hard work, but more than once I received over $20.00 for my labors for a day in the hot sun and wasp-infested barns of northwest Pike County. On Saturday, June 8, we were to put up hay for Wayne Mellon, and it was threatening rain. We just got started, and it began to pour. That ended the hay hauling for the day. I was happy as a lark because, if it rained, I had planned to go to KCCBS for the last weekend of the general camp of the Church of God (Holiness) and see Helen. She was working at the school during the summer.

I quickly went home, got ready, and pointed my Ford to Overland Park. When I arrived at the campus, the camp meeting was being blessed of the Lord. There were so many people present that there were no rooms available for Saturday night. David Churchill, my dear friend, worked as an orderly at the local hospital from 11:00 p.m. to 7:00 a.m. He offered me his bed in the boys' dorm while he worked. I gratefully received the offer and slept while he worked. Sunday afternoon I returned to Fishhook to put up hay on Monday.

I usually attended Tuesday night prayer meeting services at the Spring Valley Church where Bud McGlaughen was the pastor. I was asked to lead their prayer meeting the second week I was back from Bible school.

David Churchill, who loaned me his bed

Gary Dougherty and Dolores Leichty were married on June 21, 1968. I rode with Jerry, Judy, and Bernice Dougherty and George and Voleta Prior to Sparta, Michigan, for the wedding. We went on June 20 to be there for the rehearsal and left after the evening wedding and reception, traveling all night to get back to Fishhook. On July 4, I found myself in Overland Park watching fireworks with Helen. Then I returned to the hayfields of Pike County to make money to further my education.

Wedding of Gary Dougherty and Dolores Leichty

The Whispering Oaks Youth Camp took place in mid-August with Larry Warren as the camp evangelist. Although Gary and Dolores Dougherty were married, they still helped with the youth camp. Gary and I served as boys' monitors. We had a great youth camp with several young people seeking the Lord at the altar.

Preaching and working made for a busy summer. Soon it was time for school to start again. Helen had gone home to Ashley, Michigan, to visit her family prior to the beginning of the school year. I worked in the hayfield the day before leaving for Michigan to get Helen and go back to KCCBS. Many of you know that the most direct route from Fishhook, Illinois, to Overland Park, Kansas, is not via Ashley, Michigan, but for a young man in love, a slight detour of a thousand miles was not a problem. That was my first visit to the Denniston home. Helen's sister Becky had enrolled at

KCCBS, and the next day she traveled with us as we made our way to Kansas.

During the summer of 1968, I labored with my hands, back, and knees in the hayfields of Pike County. Saint Paul was a tent maker, and he labored at his trade to support himself as he preached the gospel. The Bible says in I Thessalonians 2:9, "For ye remember, brethren, our labour and travail: for labouring night and day, because we would not be chargeable unto any of you, we preached unto you the gospel of God." It was a privilege to work with my hands and have the Holy Spirit open many doors for me to preach the gospel.

Story 21

Starting My Sophomore Year

Because I had worked for Clark's Bus Service the previous school year, I was able to drive a bus again when school started. My classes included Personal Evangelism with R.E. Trotter, Latin with C.E. Cowen, Beginning Theology with R.E. Trotter, Early American History with Carlos Ross, and Speech with Philip Estes.

Having been a dating couple the previous semester, Helen and I had learned the system well. Couples could have an on-campus social privilege on Sunday for church. We could walk to Monday night prayer meeting slow enough to meet and walk together. Both of us ate in the dining hall and could just happen to stand together in the meal lines. It was convenient to get my mail about the same time my special friend did. Wednesday evening prayer meeting could be another on-campus date. Dating couples could sit together on Thursday for lunch. At times we would substitute the two on-campus social privileges for an off-campus one. We did our best at keeping within the school dating rules but also worked the rules to our greatest advantage.

God had helped me to complete my freshman year of college, and I was indeed thankful. The sophomore year had some academic mountains that seemed tall and challenging. I was taking my first foreign language course. Because I had a difficult time with the proper usage of the English language, Latin was very threatening to a farm boy from Fishhook. Faithfully, I attended the classes, did my best, and struggled my way through two semesters. I loved Beginning Theology, Personal Evangelism, and Early American History. Speech was something I desperately needed but never had studied in a structured way until taking the course. Philip Estes was a recent graduate, and having students like Delbert Scott, Jack Smith, Joel Riley, and Steve Manley certainly got his teaching career off to a challenging start. God was gracious, and the teachers were merciful to me.

The first nine weeks of the first semester of my sophomore year were marked by me managing to get on the Merit Honor Roll. That so overwhelmed my dear mother back at Fishhook that she sent the information to George Bridgeman who published the unbelievable news in the *Baylis Guide*, our local newspaper. I am sure to some of the local folks that it was as amazing as Orville and Wilbur Wright flying an airplane.

If I learned anything during my early days in Bible school, it was persistence. I did my best to attend my classes, read the material from the textbook, do the collateral reading, and complete the necessary term papers. The Bible says in Matthew 10:22b, "But he that endureth to the end shall be saved." I applied that to going to college and concluded that if I endured until the end, I would be graduated.

Story 22

Church Rally in Lebanon

In addition to my academic pursuits, I preached every time the Lord provided a pulpit for me to preach the gospel. Helen's sister Mary Harris and her husband, Phillip, were pastoring a Wesleyan Church in Lebanon, Indiana. I received a call from Phillip to speak at his church in a fall rally on Saturday evening and Sunday morning, October 5-6, 1968. I readily accepted the invitation, and Helen, her sister Becky, and I left KCCBS in my Ford Fairlane at 3:00 a.m. and traveled east about five hundred miles to the Harris home. Helen's mother, father, and youngest brother, Alfred, were there when we arrived at 12:30 p.m. I preached that night, and the three Denniston sisters, Helen, Becky, and Mary sang. After service we enjoyed eating fried peach pies, a Denniston family specialty.

That visit seemed to be a bit of a setup. It appeared that Helen's family all ganged up to tease us about when she and I were getting married. Pastor Harris even welcomed me into the family. It was good to get to know the Denniston family better, and I thought to myself, *Maybe someday I will become a part of this family.*

Sunday morning was a special rally for the Sunday school and church. Several unsaved people were present for the service, and, as always, the Holy Spirit was faithful to convict of sin, of righteousness, and of judgment. No one sought the Lord, but the Lord was seeking several needy souls.

After a lovely and delicious meal, I pointed the little Ford westward to 7401 Metcalf Avenue, Overland Park. I had been very careless about buying on the Lord's Day in my youth, but God had dealt with me about being careful as a Christian. Therefore, I had taken gas cans to Indiana and filled them on Saturday so that I could drive back to Overland Park on Sunday. When going around St. Louis on I-270, my Ford ran out of gas. Thankfully, I was able to get to the side of the Interstate and pour the gasoline into the tank of my car, and I did not buy on Sunday. I learned years later that had the gasoline exploded in my little Ford, all of us riding in it would have been blown to pieces. God watched over us, and we made it just fine. We arrived back at the Bible school about 11:30 p.m.

During our courtship it became clear that I was serious about being a minister. Helen came to realize that the work of the Lord was very important to me as a Bible school student and would continue to be for the rest of my life. If she did not want to hear me preach or go to church and be involved in the work of the Lord, she needed to think about dating some other fellow. Somehow those things did not frighten her away from the preacher boy from Fishhook. It seems to me that if a young man has a call to preach or to any aspect of God's work that his girlfriend or wife-to-be also should share a deep love for God and His work.

During the months that Helen and I dated, the majority of our dates were to revivals, street meetings, church services, and other spiritual functions. It was preparation for the work we would spend our lives doing. Hebrew 10:25 says, "Not forsaking the assembling of ourselves together, as the manner of some is; but exhorting one another: and so much the more, as ye see the day approaching." Helen's father was a minister of the gospel, so she was used to going to church and church functions. The man she was dating had several things in common with her preacher dad.

Story 23

Engagement

Having carefully studied the Scriptures, I believed I Timothy 3:2a, "A bishop then must be blameless, the husband of one wife." I came to the conclusion that I needed a Christian wife, and that Helen Jean Denniston was the woman God wanted me to marry.

On October 26, I traveled to the Manley farm and spent time with my family. After the noon meal on Sunday, I got my two brothers to go to their room as I wanted to talk with my parents about getting their approval to ask Helen to marry me. They were not surprised when I told them my intentions and gave their consent. One hurdle down and the second hurdle would be to get Helen to say, "Yes."

SPECIAL YOUTH SERVICES

CHURCH OF GOD (Holiness)
1108 St. Mary's Blvd.

Gospel Team from
Kansas City College and Bible School
Overland Park, Kansas

NOVEMBER 15, 16, 17, 1968

7:30 P. M. each Nite   11:00 A. M. Sunday

PREACHING — GOOD MUSIC — SINGING

EVERYBODY WELCOME ! !

Rev. James H. Alley
Pastor

 5

Announcement of youth services in Jefferson City, MO

It was a rainy Saturday night, November 2, 1968, when Helen and I went to the Christian Service Youth Rally in the school chapel for our social privilege. After the service we went to the International House of Pancakes. When we pulled into the parking lot next to the girls' dorm and parked the car, I mustered all the courage I had, and I asked Helen to marry me. She said, "I would love to." I was not sure if that was a yes or a no so I asked her again and she said, "Yes." It was about 10:20, and she had to be in the dorm at 10:30. Needless to say, we did not have much time to make wedding plans that night.

The next day Helen and I with some other students traveled to Hiawatha, Kansas. I preached twice at the Wesleyan Holiness Church. Ronald Hershberger, their pastor, was away, and I filled-in for him. We ate dinner with the Johansens and Mrs. Johansen kept calling us Brother and Sister Manley. That same day, Ruth Hosier, one of our fellow students, surprised us by asking if we were engaged. There must have been some stars in our eyes.

Students were not to make the announcement of their engagement without the permission of the Bible school officials, so on November 6, I went to President C.E. Cowen's office and asked to make the announcement. He said a committee had to give their approval, but he, being my Latin teacher, said, "I will do it *quam celerimme*" meaning "as quickly as possible." The committee gave their approval. On Thursday after sitting together for lunch, Helen and I went to Gary and Dolores' apartment and told them our special news. They gave their blessings to our engagement.

After being teased at the bus garage about getting engaged, I went to the Bible school for supper. I soon completed my meal and walked to the boys' dorm where I was met at the door by several fellows. Kenneth Marshall told me to take everything out of my pockets and to remove my belt. They then carried me to a bathroom where they lowered me into a bathtub half full of cold water. I am not sure if they were angry with me for getting engaged or just jealous. I guess I will never know for sure which was the case.

On November 15, I took a group of students to Jefferson City, Missouri, for a weekend revival at the Church of God (Holiness) Church where Reverend James Alley was the pastor. We got lost Friday night and did not arrive at the church until very late, but the people still were waiting for us. We gave our testimonies and went to the designated homes. I stayed with Reverend and Mrs. H.L. Fuller. The next morning we had creamed eggs for breakfast. That was my first exposure to that delicious treat. It is white gravy with chopped boiled eggs added to it. Grace Fuller served it over toast. Yummy! Gordon Snyder and I took turns preaching in the meeting. That weekend was a sample of what Helen and I were to experience many times in the future. For various reasons I have had to leave her behind to go somewhere and preach the gospel.

During our courtship Helen and I often read and quoted Ruth 1:16-17: "And Ruth said, Entreat me not to leave thee, or to return from following after thee: for whither thou goest, I will go; and where thou lodgest, I will lodge: thy people shall be my people, and thy God my God: Where thou diest, will I die, and there will I be buried: the LORD do so to me, and more also, if ought but death part thee and me." Although there have been times when the work of the Lord required us to be separated, we had made a commitment to each other for life. We still have that commitment today even when we have to be thousands of miles apart.

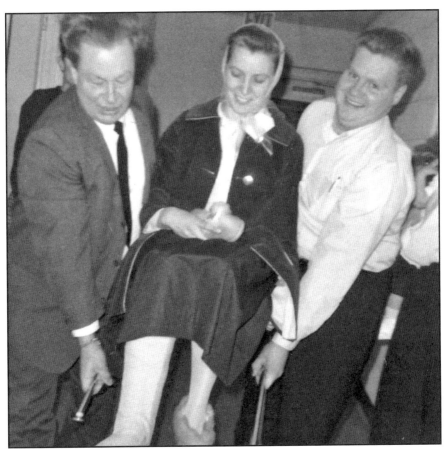

Helen Denniston being carried by Robert Carroll and me

Story 24

Christmastime in Michigan

After our engagement Helen and I began to make plans for our June wedding to take place at the Wesleyan Holiness Church in St. Louis, Michigan, which was her home church. We planned to go to Michigan at Christmastime and work on wedding preparations.

Helen was teaching physical education for the high school and college girls during the fall term. On December 12, 1968, while playing basketball, she accidentally cracked a bone in her right foot. There was a trip to the emergency room for X-rays, and then the next day a cast was applied. Another student loaned her crutches to walk. On December 20, Helen received a walking cast, and we headed to Michigan for Christmas. We were well chaperoned. Helen's sister Becky needed a ride back to Ashley. Kendra Mosher needed a ride to Cedar Springs, Michigan. Dawn Russell needed a ride to Greenville, Michigan. With a full trunk, a backseat filled with female students, and Helen with her big cast up front, I pointed the Ford northward about midday and started our eight-hundred-mile journey to Ashley.

As the miles clicked by, we all became weary, and soon my four female passengers were sleeping. It was not easy to keep awake when all of my passengers were sleeping. I had driven for perhaps six hours and it had been dark for a few hours. On two-lane US Highway 36, between Jacksonville, Illinois, and Springfield, Illinois, I dozed at the wheel and awoke meeting a semi. I was frightened! I could have been killed along with my passengers. I was wide awake for many miles after that close call. I did everything I could think of to keep awake after that experience.

When we got into Michigan, I again became very weary. Because Helen could not drive with a cast on her leg, I asked Becky to drive. She got behind the wheel and drove until we were through most of Grand Rapids. It was still dark when a policeman signaled for Becky to stop, and he asked to see her driver's license. She had a hard time finding it as she had covered it with Doug Lyon's picture.

Finally she found the license and handed it to the officer. He wanted to know where my back license plate was, and I told him that I did not know because it was on the car when we left Kansas. Then he asked to see my registration. I told him I had sent it to get new plates but that I had a license plate on the front. He looked at the front plate, checked Becky's driver's license, and told me to go to the Clark gas station up ahead, borrow a screwdriver, and put the front plate on the back. To our relief he let us go.

We stopped at the gas station as told. I got out into an extremely cold Michigan morning, and with fingers that quickly became numb, I changed the license plate. It was not much farther to Cedar Springs, and we helped Kendra unload her things. Her father gave me $5.00 for bringing his daughter from Kansas to Michigan for Christmas. In those days you could make the trip from KCCBS to Ashley for about $15.00. I drove a few more miles to Greenville where Dawn lived. Then we traveled the forty miles to Ashley.

It was good to be with Helen's family and get to know them better. At the time I did not realize fully how much her people would become my people, but I eventually made that discovery and was thankful for it. We went to the Wesleyan Holiness Church for services Sunday morning. That was my first visit to Helen's home church. Sad to say, I got sick Sunday afternoon and was not able to go to church that night. It was Monday afternoon before I was able to be up and about. My sickness shall be blamed forever on changing the front license plate to the back of my Ford in Grand Rapids on a bitter-cold Michigan morning. Early on Tuesday, the day before Christmas, I headed for Fishhook to be with my family for Christmas. On the way there the generator light came on, and I prayed my way to the Manley farm without the battery failing me.

That was to be my last Christmas with my family as a single man. I was making some great changes by taking on the responsibly of becoming a husband. My love for Helen overshadowed the transition.

I became more interested in Bible passages like Ephesians 5:25, "Husbands, love your wives, even as Christ also loved the church, and gave himself for it." It seemed that everywhere I read in the Bible, something was being said about marriage. Strange indeed!

Story 25

Second Semester of My Sophomore Year

During the first semester of my sophomore year, I dated full-time, became engaged, preached every time and everywhere the Lord opened a door, and drove a school bus. It was truly amazing grace that allowed me to complete fifteen hours.

As I enrolled for the second semester, I had a dual-track focus. I wanted to complete my studies in four years, and I wanted to get married. Although I was not a math major, I did some figuring and realized that driving a bus for $40.00 per week was not going to meet my financial obligations. I began to seek for additional income.

My friend Gary was a married student and worked for the Johnson County Library system. He thought I could get a job working five hours per day as a custodian. I contacted Ralph Beckham, father of Richard—a gifted singer, who was a supervisor at the Johnson County Library. He helped me make my way through the procedures of landing the job. After my classes at school, I worked at the library. One thing I did not like was missing supper in the dining hall. The school cooks packed lunches for the working students, and it was usually a sandwich, two cookies, and perhaps some chips. I was saving money to get married, so I did not go out to eat but thanked God for my sack lunch. I longed for the day when I would have a wife, a stove, and a refrigerator so that I could have what I wanted for supper.

The job helped me make more money, but I missed going to Wednesday night prayer meetings, revival services, and other spiritual activities. However, I kept up my devotional life and enjoyed the blessing of the Lord in my soul in spite of not being able to go to church at night during the work week. I appreciated the chapel services and other daytime spiritual activities that I attended.

Everyone's internal clock operates differently. I function well in the mornings and not well late at night. Thus at times I would set my alarm for 3:30 or 4:00 a.m. to get my school work done rather than burn the proverbial midnight oil.

As our wedding approached, I was able to transition from five hours per night to eight hours per day as a custodian. I went to work before my classes began and then returned after my afternoon classes. That way I was able to study and also attend some services in the evenings. It was a taxing schedule, but I kept my focus on my dual goals of graduating in four years and getting married at the end of my sophomore year.

The Lord has helped me over the years to focus on a goal and work at achieving it. In I Corinthians 9:24-26 it says: "Know ye not that they which run in a race run all, but one receiveth the prize? So run, that ye may obtain. And every man that striveth for the mastery is temperate in all things. Now they do it to obtain a corruptible crown; but we an incorruptible. I therefore so run, not as uncertainly; so fight I, not as one that beateth the air." My dual goals caused me to focus on making both of them happen as planned.

Are you planning to be at the Marriage Supper of the Lamb? That great event will take place as recorded in Revelation 19:7-9: "Let us be glad and rejoice, and give honor to him: for the marriage of the Lamb is come, and his wife hath made herself ready. And to her was granted that she should be arrayed in fine linen, clean and white: for the fine linen is the righteousness of saints. And he saith unto me, Write, Blessed are they which are called unto the marriage supper of the Lamb. And he saith unto me, These are the true sayings of God." Much human preparation goes into an earthly wedding, and you certainly need to prepare spiritually for the Marriage Supper of the Lamb!

Story 26

Easter Revival at New Goshen

I was busy going to college and planning for our wedding, but I did my best to preach every time God opened a door. Jane Wardle, one of my classmates, attended the Wesleyan Church in New Goshen, Indiana, just north of Terre Haute where John Steward was the pastor. He invited a group of students from KCCBS to come for an Easter weekend revival.

Eldon Manners and I were among those who went, and we rode in his and his twin brother Edwin's tan Rambler. Joanne Hosier, Jane Wardle, and Arlene McGhee went also and rode in Joanne's tan Oldsmobile. On the way to the meeting, we stopped to eat, and after the meal the ladies asked Eldon and me to help them close the trunk. The ladies were inside the car. We closed the trunk, and it popped open. We closed it, tested it to be sure it was latched, and it popped open again. That car had an inside opener, and the ladies were having a great laugh with a couple of not-so-luxury-car savvy Bible school boys. It was not until I was preparing this book that I learned that it was Arlene who was guilty of operating the trunk opener.

Eldon and I took turns preaching. We went calling on Saturday in the neighborhood, inviting people to the revival. God blessed that outreach effort to our hearts and those we invited. A little boy by the name of John McLaren came to the altar after I had preached. Many years later he attended the Wesleyan Holiness Church that I pastored in Portage, Pennsylvania, and worked for our Christian day school as a bus driver and maintenance man.

We had a sunrise service on Easter morning in New Goshen, and Eldon spoke. On the way home from the church, we stopped at a cemetery where Jane Wardle's father was buried. It was a sunshiny morning, and I was surprised to see several people in the cemetery early on Easter morning.

Helen came from Michigan with her sister Becky and her boyfriend Doug Lyon, and Helen was in the services on Sunday.

Joanne loaned us her car that night so Helen and I could travel back to KCCBS together. We were followed by Eldon and the other ladies in his car. It was a long trip, and we got to the Bible school campus after 4:00 a.m. I was very weary, having driven all the way from New Goshen, and I went quickly to my room and was soon fast asleep. Within a little over an hour, someone knocked on my door telling me that I had a call on the pay phone down the hall. The person whom I had arranged to cover for me at work that day did not show up. I had to stagger over to the Johnson County Library and dump the wastebaskets and clean the rest rooms. I went through the motions but was dead on my feet.

I have known secular college students who partied well into the early morning hours and then were unable to go to classes because they were spaced out on drugs or drunk with alcohol. I had preached the gospel and was sober, but I was not up to going to classes that morning.

There is great joy in serving the Lord Jesus Christ, and as a young minister I really enjoyed working with other young people in special services. Jesus said in John 15:11, "These things have I spoken unto you, that

Doug Lyon courting Becky Denniston

my joy might remain in you, and that your joy might be full." The inward joy of serving Jesus Christ has no equal. The greatest joy that one can know is the joy of salvation. The angels themselves have great joy when a sinner repents. Luke 15:10 says, "Likewise, I say unto you, there is joy in the presence of the angels of God over one sinner that repenteth." Going forth with the good news of salvation is wonderful. Moreover, to witness the conversion of a sinner to Jesus Christ truly is a joyful experience.

Story 27

Helen's Graduation

Helen had a busy spring in 1969. She was planning our wedding plus her own graduation from college. We certainly were living in the fast lane. I enrolled in a class in college called The Family taught by Erskine Hughes. Helen wanted to take it, too, but did not need the credit and did not have time to do all the collateral reading required, so she audited the class. It was helpful to both of us as we prepared for marriage.

As our wedding day drew near, I began to seek for an affordable place to live. We had a small amount of furniture and wanted to keep housing costs as low as possible. I heard about the little house at 8226 Johnson Drive in Merriam, Kansas. Other students had lived there, so I checked about it. To a farm boy from Fishhook, it

Steve, Doug, Becky, and Helen's parents in the kitchen of the rented house

looked like a remodeled chicken house. It had one bedroom, a living room, kitchen, and bathroom. The house was completely furnished, was available for $65.00 per month, and was located close to the Johnson County Library branch where I was employed. I rented the house for the month of May to secure it for our use after our June 7 wedding.

May 28, 1969, was graduation day at KCCBS. Helen's parents came from Michigan for that special event and stayed in our rented house. It was their only visit to Kansas while we lived there.

Helen had been a good student in college and graduated with honors. Three of her fellow classmates did well, also. Eldon and Edwin Manners—identical twins, Harold Blair, and Helen were the top students.

Helen with her college diploma

Reverend and Mrs. Charles Denniston, Helen, and Becky left for Michigan the day after graduation and stopped by the Harry Manley farm and stayed the night. After the Denniston family left for Michigan, I moved from the boys' dorm into our home on Johnson Drive. I was terribly lonely staying by myself, but I was there only a few days before I headed to Michigan for our wedding.

It is important to set goals and important to achieve them. Helen had a God-given desire to go to Bible college and made many sacrifices to accomplish her goal. She started her college training at Ebenezer Bible School in Vestaburg, Michigan. While attending Ebenezer, she worked at the Wolverine Shoe Factory in Ithaca to support herself. Then she bravely left Michigan and went to KCCBS to complete her degree.

Helen's first roommate in the girls' dorm was Judith Hauck who married Ronald Hershberger in June 1967. Susan Olsen, her second roommate, married Philip Estes in December 1967, after she and Helen roomed together one semester. Her third roommate, Dolores Leichty married Gary Dougherty in June of 1968. Needless to say, with such a reputation, there was a long list of young ladies who wanted to room with her. Her fourth roommate was her sister Becky, who married Doug Lyon a little more than six months after Helen and I were married.

Helen received her Bachelor of Arts degree from KCCBS. Just eleven days later she got her MRS degree from John Stevan Manley. The Bible says in Proverbs 2:10-12: "When wisdom entereth into thine heart, and knowledge is pleasant unto thy soul; Discretion shall preserve thee, understanding shall keep thee: To deliver thee from the way of the evil man, from the man that speaketh froward things."

Story 28

Dorm Deals

As I prepared to move out of the boys' dorm, I certainly did not want to fail to pack the memories of some unforgettable dorm deals. Please permit me to share a few.

Shoe polish: Going to Bible school with limited financial backing resulted in most of the guys having a limited amount of footwear. Using only one or two pair of shoes caused them to get scuffed and in need of a good polishing on Saturday before that evening's social privilege and the Sunday church services. I recall one Saturday polishing my shoes in the lobby of the boys' dorm and a friend asking to borrow my polish. I let him take the polish and went on to do other things. A few days passed by, perhaps more than a week, and I needed to polish my shoes. I asked the fellow for my polish. He had loaned it to his friend. That friend loaned it to another friend. When I got the can back, the bottom of it was shining, and there was not much polish left in the can. Lesson learned: DO NOT POLISH SHOES IN THE LOBBY!

A very big catch: The boys' dorm was an old building that at one time had been used as a mental institution. The basement was indeed an eerie place. Because of the age of the building, there were some unwelcome residents in the dorm. Preparing food in your room was greatly restricted by school rules. You could pop popcorn, but that was about all you could prepare. I had some popcorn in my room, and a mouse thought it was just as tasty as I did and helped himself to my supply. Being a farm boy from Fishhook, I considered myself a skilled trapper. I soon had a mouse trap baited and was ready to tan the hide of Mr. Mouse. The trap went off shortly after I got into bed. When I turned on the light, I was shocked to find that the bait had attracted a huge roach, and he had been killed in the mouse trap. Knowing that no one would believe such a thing happened, I went next door in the dorm and showed David Brixy the roach in the trap. I wish I had taken a photo of it. It certainly was a big roach. Lesson learned: WHEN YOU BAIT A TRAP, YOU NEVER KNOW WHAT YOU WILL CATCH!

Night monitor's full room: Working as the night monitor was a way of helping to reduce one's school bill, but it often led to making a few people unhappy with you. One of my friends worked in that capacity and someone decided to fill his room with unused dorm furniture while he was on a date. They found beds, dressers, and mattresses to fill his room. He came in from his date at the appointed hour, and boys were hiding in other rooms expecting him to blow a fuse when he saw the mess in his room. He took the prank with a great spirit and a good attitude and really disappointed the pranksters. Come to find out, the fellow had gotten engaged that night, and his spirits were soaring with the eagles. Lesson learned: KEEP A GOOD ATTITUDE WHEN BAD THINGS HAPPEN!

Electric alarm clocks: I personally never trusted an electric alarm clock. I just knew the power would fail, and I would be late. When I was in Bible school, I trusted an old-fashioned wind-up alarm clock. One of the fellows from the South had a great deal of confidence in the electric alarm clock and its ability to not run down like my old wind-up alarm clock. The big problem was that he could sleep through the alarm, but none of his neighbors could. Many mornings the alarm would awaken everyone in that hall but him. Finally, someone would pound on his door until he shut it off. Lesson learned: "LOVE NOT SLEEP LEST THOU COME TO POVERTY" (Proverbs 20:13).

Fire in the dorm: One cold winter night a student who worked second shift plugged in his electric blanket before he went to work. Something malfunctioned and it started a fire. The fire department was called, and the mattress was thrown out the second-floor window of the boys' dorm and landed near my first-floor room. I knew nothing about the fire until the next morning at breakfast. Lesson learned: "I WILL BOTH LAY ME DOWN IN PEACE, AND SLEEP: FOR THOU, LORD, ONLY MAKEST ME DWELL IN SAFETY" (Psalms 4:8).

Story 29

Wedding and Honeymoon

It was a long countdown of days from our engagement on November 2, 1968, but at last we rapidly were approaching our wedding day on June 7, 1969. I left work at the Johnson County Library and traveled to the Manley farm on June 5. My parents and two brothers, Rodney and Len, loaded their things into the Manley Chevy. I loaded my belongings into my little Ford, and we traveled northward to Michigan. My parents each told me it was not too late to back out, but I had no intention of doing so.

We had the rehearsal on Friday evening, June 6, at the Wesleyan Holiness Church of St. Louis, Michigan. My family stayed with Helen's sister Marjorie Hodges and her husband, Robert, and their children. They also housed the groom—me! Bob and Marge graciously prepared the rehearsal meal and served it at the American Legion Hall in St. Louis, the same building we used for our wedding reception.

Rev. and Mrs. Charles Denniston
request the honor of your presence
at the marriage of their daughter
Helen Jean
to
Mr. John Stevan Manley
on Saturday, the seventh of June
Nineteen hundred and sixty-nine
at two-thirty o'clock in the afternoon
the Lord willing
Wesleyan Holiness Church
419 Center Street
St. Louis, Michigan

Our wedding announcement

The day of our wedding was a lovely, sunshiny June day. I must have been very nervous because I refused to eat dinner before our wedding. In my mind the wedding was picture perfect. Reverend Marvin Reiff officiated. Dawn Russell sang "Because You Come to Me," "Whither Thou Goest," and "O Perfect Love." We exchanged vows, promising to be faithful until death. I claimed the lovely

Helen and me on our wedding day

bride with a kiss, and we walked down the aisle as Reverend and
Mrs. John Stevan Manley.

As we descended the steps from the church, I slipped on the rice,
and Helen held me to keep me from falling. She has faithfully held
me up ever since. After the reception and opening the gifts, we tried
to leave for our honeymoon. Rocks had been placed in the hubcaps

and had to be removed. Some newly acquired mischievous brothers-in-law put Limburger cheese on the manifold, but we burned it off without noticing any odor as we drove toward Niagara Falls.

Being mindful of the rapidly approaching Lord's Day, we got a motel room at Stevens Motel in Lapeer, Michigan, for Saturday and Sunday nights. We also purchased some food to eat on Sunday. Reverend Dorland Loomis was the pastor of the United Holiness Church in Lapeer and his wife, Ruth, was the pianist for our wedding. We did not find their church for Sunday morning but attended the local Church of the Nazarene. Sunday afternoon I called the Loomis home and got directions so we could worship with them in the evening. After the service we were invited to the parsonage for an enjoyable snack and visit with the Loomis family.

Monday we traveled from Lapeer to Niagara Falls taking the Canadian route. We passed through customs at Sarnia, Ontario, Canada, then drove on the Queen Elizabeth Highway to the Falls. My father tried to find out where we were going on our honeymoon by telling us they would be diverting the Falls for repairs. I made only a passing noncommittal comment about it. Arriving in the afternoon from the Canadian side, we saw Niagara Falls in its entire splendor. It was truly breathtaking to behold. We checked into Gulliver's Queensway Motel three minutes from the Falls. It was at that motel that I removed the charred remains of the Limburger cheese that was still on the manifold. We returned to the Falls after dark to view the lovely colored lights displayed on the Falls. It was truly an awesome sight—almost as lovely as my newly acquired wife.

After visiting Niagara Falls, we returned to Ashley where we loaded Helen's belongings and our gifts into the little Ford and left on June 12 for Fishhook. Near Bloomington, Illinois, we saw a woman standing in the median. I pulled over and asked if we could help her. She had run out of gasoline in her Cadillac and wanted us to take her to her husband who was working at a construction site. I explained that someone at the gas station up ahead would help her, and we would be happy to take her there. Because the back seat of the Ford was filled with wedding gifts, she slid into the front seat with Helen and me. As we drove to the service station, she told us her husband always put the gas in the car, and she never did that sort of thing. We decided that we would allow Helen to put gas in our car any time it was needed. That night we stayed with my family on the farm. The next day we went to our first home at 8226 Johnson Drive where I carried my bride across the threshold before unloading the Ford.

Standing on the front porch of our first home

We were on a limited budget, so we used our dollar-bill stretcher to the maximum on our honeymoon. Looking back on the prices in 1969 makes them seem laughable. Our most expensive meal in a restaurant for the two of us was a grand total of $3.85. We spent four nights in motels and the most expensive one was $9.45 with taxes included. The costliest fill-up of gasoline, with someone else pumping, was only $5.15. Our total expenses from the time we left the reception until we arrived at our first home were $99.59. I was just a young holiness preacher with my new wife, but we were determined to mind God and fulfill a God-given call to labor in His harvest field and make the sacrifices necessary to do it.

The Bible makes it clear that a bishop is not to be "greedy of filthy lucre" (I Timothy 3:3). Helen and I have not been greedy of filthy lucre, but we have tried to stretch our money as far as possible. God truly has been our dollar-bill stretcher. Praise the Lord!

Story 30

Our Busy Summer

After our wedding we returned to our jobs. Helen worked part-time in the commissary at Kings Food Host, and I worked at the Johnson County Library. It was a little challenging to make the work connections with only one car. I purchased a three-speed Western Flyer bike at a garage sale for $15.00 and rode it to work and home for lunch. That way Helen had the car to go to work in the mornings; she did not work in the afternoons.

Newlyweds in front of the United Brethren Church in Fishhook

Gary Dougherty was pastoring the Sny Church of God Independent Holiness Church that summer. The church was in a building program and was meeting at a church in Atlas, Illinois. Gary asked me to hold a revival for him the weekend of July 4. Helen and I went to the revival and spent the first night with Gary and Dolores and then went to Fishhook and stayed with my parents. July 4 always was celebrated at the Sny church with an all-day meeting. Reverend and Mrs. Raymond Shelhorn, missionaries to Japan, and their son Sam were there for the day. I shall never forget the Sunday night service of that meeting. A very strong thunderstorm came up during the service. When I stood to preach, the lights went out, and I preached my little message in the dark. When I finished preaching, the lights came back on. Helen and I traveled back to Kansas through many thunderstorms that

79

Rev. and Mrs. Raymond Shelhorn

night. Some cars had pulled off the road, but our little Ford splashed its way through the storms.

An invitation came to preach in a weekend youth revival with another young minister as my co-worker. It was a small church located about one hundred sixty-five miles from our home. My wife and I traveled to the church, and I preached the services that were assigned to me. I made a big blunder when I was preaching about Abraham praying for Sodom. I mispronounced the word peradventure. After the service I received proper instruction about the correct pronunciation should I ever preach from that passage again. Many were the times that I was humiliated and humbled because of pitiful reading skills, but God gave me grace and help. Praise the Lord!

The offering from the meeting was $15.00 for the trip of over three hundred thirty miles. Thankfully, we bought gas for 15 cents per gallon, the lowest that I ever paid for gas. Our gracious heavenly Father was watching out for us.

My wife and I traveled so much the summer we were married that we only ate Sunday dinner at home once between our wedding day and Labor Day weekend. The oil in our little Ford seldom got cold.

Neil Armstrong walked on the moon on the only Sunday we were at home that summer.

One day we stopped by the campus of KCCBS to get our mail. I went to the business office and enjoyed chatting with Carlos Ross, the business manager, while Helen went to another area of the campus. Carlos mentioned that his wife was changing jobs, and he wondered if Helen would be interested in taking the job as book-keeper at the Bible school. When Helen came by the business office, he talked with her and gave her time to think and pray about it. In the mail we received that day was another surprise offer. Helen received a letter from Carolina Christian Academy in Thomasville, North Carolina, asking her to consider coming there to teach. We prayed about those options and felt that God would have my wife work in the business office at KCCBS. That way I would be able to complete my studies, too.

That job provided on-campus housing in a third-floor apart-ment across the street from the business office. Also I received a 50 percent discount on my tuition. Although the pay was not much, the benefits were appealing. We moved onto the campus from 8226 Johnson Drive on a Saturday and then traveled to Bartlesville, Oklahoma, that evening. The Lord gave me strength to preach both times on Sunday. We came home to our apartment after the eve-ning service and awoke the next morning in a room filled with boxes.

During the trip to the Quincy youth camp that summer, our Ford developed a fuel pump leak. I look back on that and realize how serious it was to have gasoline leaking from the fuel pump and still be driv-ing the car. Thankfully, the angels of the Lord had fire extinguishers with them, and we did not have a fire, but oh, how foolish I was to push on without stop-

Flat tires as well as fuel pump problems on our Ford

ping to get the car repaired. Acts 17:30a says, "And the times of this ignorance God winked at." I got the fuel pump repaired in Illinois before returning to Kansas.

Helen knew during our time of courtship that the work of the Lord was important to me and that I would do my best to fulfill my calling. We certainly started our marriage with a very active summer of Christian service. Psalm 126:5-6 reads: "They that sow in tears shall reap in joy. He that goeth forth and weepeth, bearing precious seed, shall doubtless come again with rejoicing, bringing his sheaves with him."

Story 31

My Junior Year

After working forty hours per week and traveling somewhere to preach all but one Sunday during the summer of 1969, I was ready to get back into the classroom. When I went to enroll for the fall term, the wise counselor stated that to work a forty-hour week at Johnson County Library and carry fifteen hours of college credits would be very challenging. I was determined to graduate in four years and get into the work of the Lord, so I quit my job and started driving a school bus again. That way I could carry a full load of classes. I had two years of college behind me and two more ahead of me.

Classes for the fall were Church History with Omar Lee, History of the Far East with Richard Carroll, Principles of Sociology with Erskine Hughes, Recent U.S. History with Richard Carroll, Comparative Religions with R.E. Trotter, and Physical Education with David Newberry. It was a good semester, and I enjoyed my classes. Church History with Omar Lee was especially enlightening as I learned about the way God has worked from the birth of Jesus down through history. Omar Lee was a godly man and had a positive influence upon the lives of his students through his long and colorful career at KCCBS. I am a better man for having known him early in my life.

We were living on campus. Helen was working in the business office, and I was taking a full college load and preaching every time the Lord opened a place for me to preach. We had a full schedule, but by driving a bus I was able to attend prayer meetings and revival services in the evenings.

That was my first year as a married student. I no longer ate my meals from trays in the dining hall but enjoyed the fine meals prepared by my gourmet cook and wife. Many times we traveled together to preaching engagements and to attend services. One evening we planned to attend a revival where Reverend Winfield Poe was the evangelist. Realizing the need for praying for the revival, I felt that I should go to the school chapel and pray for the service. Tom Peak was married now and not living on campus, so I could not pray with him. On the way across the parking lot to the chapel, God spoke to me, "Your wife has worked all day in the business office. She has dishes to do, and she needs your help. Go back and help her with the dishes, and then the two of you pray together." Wow! I was not going to pray but do dishes with my wife and then pray with her! Amazing! I knew it was the voice of the Lord. I turned around, ascended the stairs, got my hands in the dishwater, and helped her do the dishes; then we prayed together. That was not the only time I have helped her do the dishes.

Did someone say, "The couple that prays together stays together"? It has worked for Helen and me. Many have been the times we have lifted our hearts together to the Lord Jesus Christ in prayer, and He has graciously answered prayer. Thank the Lord!

There is an interesting verse in I Peter 3:7. It says, "Likewise, ye husbands, dwell with them according to knowledge, giving honour unto the wife, as unto the weaker vessel, and as being heirs together of the grace of life; that your prayers be not hindered." There is great prayer power available to the husband and wife who will take advantage of it. The husband's prayers should not be hindered by a lack of love and consideration for his wife.

Story 32

Working with Carl

During my years as a student at KCCBS, Carl Myers was the Superintendent of the Buildings and Grounds. We developed a great relationship and friendship. There were times when Carl needed an extra pair of hands, and he asked me to come to his aid. We got along well and did many jobs together.

On one occasion Carl needed help painting an apartment in the girls' dorm. I put on my grubby painting clothes and joined him. It was during the winter months when funds were low at the Bible school, and he was instructed to get by with as little expense as possible. We went to the supply room where there were several cans of different colors and varied amounts of paint. Soon lids were popped from the cans, and a five-gallon bucket was receiving the partial contents of one can after another. He said that we had to mix as much as we needed because we never could match the color if we finished the paint before the job was completed. Somehow a lovely blue color resulted from the various contents, and soon the apartment was freshly painted in "Empty-Paint-Can Blue."

I was amazed at the way Carl could fix, build, and stretch things. He was the ideal man to have as the Superintendent of the Buildings and Grounds at a holiness Bible school.

My friend drove a school bus to supplement his income, and as he traveled he looked for dead trees that needed to be cut down. Later, he stopped by the house and submitted a bid for removing the tree. Several times he asked me to help him with the job. He was the chainsaw operator, and I loaded the branches and large pieces into a trailer. On a good Saturday I would make as much money helping with tree trimming as I did for driving a school bus all week. It was a good way to make extra money, and I loved working outdoors. It was a win-win for both Carl and me.

I certainly was not a skilled carpenter, but Carl was. At times I assisted him by handing building materials to him when he was on a ladder or scaffold. It was always a pleasure to work with him.

When my Ford had fuel pump problems over the Christmas break, Carl helped me get my little Ford patched up and back on the road. It was bitter cold, and we worked on the car in the school garage.

The Bible says in Proverbs 17:17a, "A friend loveth at all times," and in Proverbs 18:24 we read, "A man that hath friends must shew himself friendly: and there is a friend that sticketh closer than a brother." It was wonderful to have a multitalented friend like Carl during my college years. Over recent years we have been separated by many miles, but whenever we have the opportunity to get together, we enjoy each other's fellowship. There is a friend, the Lord Jesus Christ, who sticketh closer than a brother, and we can always enjoy His friendship and fellowship.

Story 33

Going to Callao

As a ministerial student I was often asked to fill the pulpit for pastors who were away. Reverend Richard Beckham pastored the Valley Chapel Church of God (Holiness) Church near Callao, Missouri, when I was an upperclassman. I was asked to fill his pulpit on a couple occasions. It was about one hundred fifty miles one way to the church from our apartment. My wife and I left Overland Park early in the morning, and I preached both morning and evening at the lovely little country church. The people were from rural north central Missouri, and many of them had farm backgrounds. I loved sharing the Word of God with them.

My little Ford had a small gas tank and a fuel range of about three hundred miles or a little less. The first time I went to Callao, I went prepared with a full gas can so that I would not have to purchase gasoline on the Lord's Day. The second time I filled in for Reverend Beckham, my wife and I were guests in the home of a family a few miles from the church. I was not adequately prepared for the gas the extra miles consumed. As we entered the metropolitan Kansas City area, my gas gauge began to register empty. We had many miles to travel across the large city to reach our apartment. Helen and I prayed and asked the Lord to bless the gas and help us to make it home without having to purchase gasoline. The Lord answered prayer, and we arrived safely and parked the Ford in its regular spot.

The next morning I asked Doug Lyon to drive his car to the bus garage as I was very low on gas. He agreed, and I rode to and from the bus garage with him that day. After my afternoon bus run, I got into my Ford to go for gas. It did not start, and I realized that it was completely out of gas. I took a gas can to a filling station a block away, bought gas, put it in the tank, then drove to the station and filled it. I have heard people say when the gas in their tank was very low, "We made it in on the fumes." I truly can say that was the case the Sunday night we drove home from Callao.

There might be an emergency when the ox gets into the ditch, and you have to make a purchase on the Lord's Day. On the other hand, I was so careless about not respecting the Lord's Day in my youth that I have done my best to keep it holy since my conversion. The first century Christians observed the first day of the week as the Christian Sabbath, in honor of the resurrection of the Lord Jesus Christ. I have done my best to follow their example.

The Bible says in Exodus 20:8-11: "Remember the sabbath day, to keep it holy. Six days shalt thou labour, and do all thy work: But the seventh day is the sabbath of the LORD thy God: in it thou shalt not do any work, thou, nor thy son, nor thy daughter, thy manservant, nor thy maidservant, nor thy cattle, nor thy stranger that is within thy gates: For in six days the LORD made heaven and earth, the sea, and all that in them is, and rested the seventh day: wherefore the LORD blessed the sabbath day, and hallowed it." It is my desire to honor the Lord's Day and keep it holy by not doing unnecessary business or labor on that special day.

Story 34

Senior Year Begins

One of the many blessings of my senior year at KCCBS was the return of Leroy S. Adams, Sr. to the teaching staff. Leroy had been my teacher, barber, and friend during my freshman year. It was great to have him and his wife back on campus. The front porch area of the music/staff house where they lived had many windows, and Esther Adams placed inexpensive plastic curtains over them. I heard her say, "Plastic curtains are good enough for pilgrims." Those words touched my heart, coming from a Bible school teacher's wife, who was a senior citizen and had sacrificed many years for her beloved husband to stay in Christian education.

Among the new students who enrolled at KCCBS was a fifty-year-old Korean man named Kim Yong Yun. He became acquainted with Dr. Dale Yocum when he taught in South Korea, and Dr. Yocum encouraged him to come to KCCBS. Kim sought the will of his heavenly Father about that and also sought his earthly father's permission. He received approval from both and came to KCCBS. When he was shown to his room, he stated that he had never slept on a bed. Previously, he had slept on a mat on the floor in South Korea. He especially liked rice when it was served in the dining hall. Kim had many adjustments to make here in the States; one in particular was that he would not shake hands with women. He said, "No shaky hands with the opposite sexy."

A humorous thing happened when the fellows from the boys' dorm were talking one evening soon after Kim had arrived. Ben Colburn asked him if he had any hobbies. He said he liked karate and jujitsu. Ben askcd if he could flip someone as large as he was, and before Ben knew what had happened, he was lying on the grass looking up at Kim who was saying, "Big ones easy! Big ones easy!"

I continued to drive a school bus for Clark's Bus Service, and Helen still worked as the school bookkeeper for Carlos Ross, the business manger. We lived in the upstairs apartment, and I had many opportunities to preach on Sundays. I was very thankful to be a college senior at last. The goal of graduating was now only a few months away. After graduation I planned to enter full-time ministry. I was happy to take the remaining courses that would lead me to the desired goal.

That fall I enrolled in General Psychology and American Government with Erskine Hughes, Philosophy with Dale Yocum, School Organization and Administration and Educational Foundations with Burl McClanahan. Those courses did not seem geared to being a preacher, but I had started out for a Bachelor of Arts degree, and those were courses that fell into place for my degree. Many years later I saw God was indeed at work, and I knew it not.

The chapel services were special times for me. I enjoyed hearing the various speakers who spoke in chapel. The spiritual instruction was helpful and enlightening. It was an honor to serve on the chapel committee on various occasions and make phone calls to some area pastors, inviting them to speak to the student body. In addition to the spiritual help gleaned from the speakers, I also strove to learn from each speaker about how to say things properly. There was a time or two that I learned what not to do. However, most of the time the observations were positive, and I found excellent patterns to follow. Looking back over the many years that have elapsed since I was in chapel services, I am sure the things I learned about preaching from various chapel speakers were important in my ministerial preparation.

After living in Overland Park for three years, I had learned the city well. Being a bus driver allowed me to become familiar with the area and surrounding suburbs. I was still a farm boy from Fishhook who preferred the wide open spaces of rural America to the big city. It was my secret wish to pastor a country church.

I am thankful that God placed in my heart a desire to complete my degree in four years and make whatever adjustments for it to happen. The Bible says in Hebrews 12:1, "Wherefore seeing we also are compassed about with so great a cloud of witnesses, let us lay aside every weight, and the sin which doth so easily beset us, and let us run with patience the race that is set before us." When I enrolled at KCCBS as a college freshman, the goal of graduation seemed light years away, but God helped me to complete assignment after assignment, test after test, term paper after term paper, and now I could see graduation just a few months down the way. By the grace and help of Jesus, I had run with patience the race that was set before me, and soon I would be crossing the finish line.

Story 35

Serving as Pastor from Afar

On a cold, rainy November night in 1970, Dr. Dale Yocum, the president of KCCBS, knocked on our apartment door. He had received a phone call from someone wanting to talk with me. He had Reverend Russell Ulrich's name and phone number written on a piece of paper. I did not know Reverend Ulrich, and he did not know how to get in touch with me, so he went to the highest official of the college and sent me a message by him.

I had no idea about the nature of the call, so I quickly made contact with Reverend Ulrich. He was the District Superintendent of the North Central District of the Wesleyan Holiness Association of Churches. A pastor was needed in Peoria, and he wanted me to preach to those precious people when I was in Illinois visiting my parents. I arranged to go there on the Sunday after Thanksgiving.

District Superintendent Russell Ulrich, and his wife, who asked me to go to Peoria as a fill-in

The church proved to be a small mission-type church at 1926 Lincoln Avenue in Peoria. It was a basement church in a very rough part of town. My father's good friend from the army, O.J. "KY" Oldham lived in Peoria Heights, and our family visited him many times. When I thought of Peoria, I thought of bars, booze, and breweries. A few blocks from the Oldhams' home was the large Pabst Brewery. Along the Illinois River was the Hiram Walker Distillery. To a farm boy from Fishhook, it seemed that every other building was a dimly lit bar. That certainly was not the place I would have chosen to preach, let alone pastor. However, I consented to help the church by filling

91

their pulpit. We were guests in the home of Francis and Melba Lee that weekend.

After that first visit I received a follow-up phone call from Reverend Ulrich asking that I preach again in Peoria. I consented and in due process of time, I was asked to be the pastor of the little church. As I prayed about it, I sensed that I should continue my studies at KCCBS and graduate, but I was willing to drive from Overland Park to Peoria once per month until I had graduated. The people accepted that arrangement.

Helen and I traveled to my parents' home on Friday night after work, a four-and-a-half-hour drive, and spent the night with them. Then on Saturday afternoon or evening we traveled two hours to the Lees' home in East Peoria and spent the night. We had Sunday school and church. Following the noon meal we had an afternoon service after which Helen and I traveled back to my parents' home, got the gas I had stored there, and returned to the Bible school. It was about three hundred seventy miles one way and took us at least seven hours.

The snow tires on my little Ford were in poor condition, so I purchased some new ones at Montgomery Ward. During the month of March, a major winter storm moved across Kansas on Sunday. Francis Lee heard the weather report and suggested that the afternoon service be cancelled. After the midday meal, Helen and I headed to Fishhook. My parents were concerned about the heavy snow being reported across Missouri, but after I filled the Ford, that time from Dad's fuel tank, we started to Overland Park in the late afternoon.

Soon after we got on the road, the snow started falling or I should say dumping. By the time we arrived in Hannibal, Missouri, thirty miles away, cars were spinning out on the hills. I kept the Ford pointed directly into the storm while cars and trucks were sliding into the ditches. A snowplow even went into the ditch. We went south to I-70 in an attempt to find a better road, but even the interstate was in a poor condition on which to travel.

My precious mother was worried sick about us and kept trying to call our apartment. Cell phones were unheard of in March 1971. The Bible says in Proverbs 18:10, "The name of the LORD is a strong tower: the righteous runneth into it, and is safe." We truly prayed our way across Missouri that night. Thanking God for those new snow tires and for His mercy, we arrived at our campus apartment in the midst of a major snowstorm. I am not sure how many inches of snow were on the ground, but I would guess about twelve. The trip that normally took us four and a half hours took us seven hours. After the challenge of driving through the blizzard, we awoke the next morning to discover the schools were closed and neither Helen nor I had to work. We had pushed on but really had not needed to endanger our lives. We were thankful for God's great mercy in spite of our lack of wisdom.

Story 36

A Pure and Burning Heart

The Lord Jesus Christ said in Matthew 5:8, "Blessed are the pure in heart: for they shall see God." After giving my heart to Jesus Christ and becoming a born-again believer, I became aware of something on the inside that at times did not feel right and, if not held down, did not act right. That carnal thing was not like Jesus Christ. I did my best to suppress it, but I knew something more was needed in my innermost being. I read in Romans 8:6-7: "For to be carnally minded is death; but to be spiritually minded is life and peace. Because the carnal mind is enmity against God: for it is not subject to the law of God, neither indeed can be."

That old nature in me came from fallen Adam, having been passed from generation to generation. I needed that old nature removed by the purging work of the Holy Spirit. Jesus made it clear in Matthew 15:18-19: "But those things which proceed out of the mouth come forth from the heart; and they defile the man. For out of the heart proceed evil thoughts, murders, adulteries, fornications, thefts, false witness, blasphemies." As I searched the Scriptures and listened to Holy Ghost-anointed preachers, I came to realize that the infilling of the Holy Spirit included purifying the heart of the believer. Peter testified about that happening to the Gentiles who assembled at the home of Cornelius. Acts 15:8-9 states: "And God, which knoweth the hearts, bare them witness, giving them the Holy Ghost, even as he did unto us; And put no difference between us and them, purifying their hearts by faith."

In addition to the purifying aspect of the infilling of the Holy Spirit, I became aware of the need of power from the Holy Spirit to witness. In Acts 1:8 Jesus said, "But ye shall receive power, after that the Holy Ghost is come upon you: and ye shall be witnesses unto me both in Jerusalem, and in all Judaea, and in Samaria, and unto the uttermost part of the earth." I realized that the Holy Spirit was sent to empower the disciples to witness for the Lord Jesus Christ and bring the lost to Him.

The Church of God (Holiness) Church on 27th Street in Kansas City purchased a house on a large lot in South Park, Kansas. We remodeled the house to use temporarily as a place of worship, planning to build a church later. A revival was planned with Reverend H.E. Darnell for late November and early December 1970, but because of the lack of an appropriate place to hold those services, they were conducted at the Rosedale Church of God (Holiness) Church were Reverend Richard Payne was the pastor.

Evangelist Darnell was known for his pointed holiness preaching and for asking for a show of hands during the altar service of those who were saved and then asking the same for those who knew that they were sanctified wholly. The Holy Spirit made it clear to me during those services that I needed to be entirely sanctified. I sought God with all my heart. I asked Him to remove every carnal thing from my heart. I yielded everything to Jesus Christ that night. Without reservation I put up the white flag of surrender to the lordship of Jesus Christ. I prayed and wept at the altar until I felt emptied of selfish ambitions and carnal desires. The Apostle Paul said it like this in II Corinthians 7:1, "Having therefore these promises, dearly beloved, let us cleanse ourselves from all filthiness of the flesh and spirit, perfecting holiness in the fear of God." By the grace of God, I did my best to do just that.

Helen and I left the church that night, December 1, 1970, and on the way home the Holy Spirit spoke to me, "I will never leave thee nor forsake thee." I immediately became aware of the cleansing work of the Holy Spirit and a deep peace in my soul. I knew the Holy Spirit had come to abide.

A few days later I preached at the Belton, Missouri, Church of God (Holiness) Church, and the Holy Spirit convicted of sin and of righteousness and of judgment. We had an altar service that night, and people were saved, and others were sanctified. God placed His seal of approval upon what He had done in my heart when the Holy Spirit came in purity and power. All glory and praise to Him.

I am so glad for the infilling of the Holy Spirit. We holiness people call it entire sanctification. Some use the biblical term baptized with the Holy Spirit. Amos Binney defines entire sanctification as follows: "Entire sanctification is the act of the Holy Ghost whereby the justified soul is made holy. This instantaneous work of the

Sanctifier is usually preceded and followed by a gradual growth in grace" (*Binney's Theological Compend*, p.129).

For many years my father owned a John Deere A. It was a two-cylinder tractor that was sometimes called a Johnny Popper because of the unique sound it made from the two-cylinder system. The infilling of the Holy Spirit or entire sanctification has something that can be compared to that old tractor. To be a true New Testament Christian, one needs two cylinders operating down in the soul. Those two cylinders are purity and power. With them operating under the leadership of the Holy Spirit, the believer can be a successful witness for the Lord.

Story 37

Speaking in a Chapel Service

Many times when I was a student, my wife and I were out of town on Sunday for me to preach, and we arrived back on campus late Sunday night or early Monday morning. On one memorable occasion I had preached at the Sny Church of God Independent Holiness Church near Louisiana, Missouri. After the service Helen and I traveled back to KCCBS. We arrived very late, and I failed to set the alarm on the clock before going to bed.

My brother-in-law Doug Lyon and his wife, Becky, lived in the apartment below ours on the Bible school campus. Doug Lyon, Jack Smith, Gayle Woods, Richard Carroll, and I rode to the bus barn together. On that particular Monday morning we were not moving the kitchen chairs above the Lyons' apartment, and it was only a few minutes before we were to leave. Doug knocked on our door and awakened me. I had overslept. I hurriedly dressed, putting on my suit, white shirt, and tie because I was to preach in chapel immediately after my bus run. I had no time to shave or eat breakfast but quickly dashed off to drive my bus.

About three or four blocks from the junior high school where I was to unload my passengers, the engine quit on the bus. In those days there were no cell phones, so I had to get off the bus and go to a house to call the bus garage for help. While I was out of the bus, a woman driving a station wagon tried to go around the bus and caved in both doors on one side of her car. I then needed to have the police come and fill out an accident report. After too many minutes had passed, I got another bus and made it back to the campus.

I was late for the chapel service, and dear Dr. Burl McClanahan was pacing in the back of the chapel, longing for my entry. He was delighted when I arrived, not necessarily because I was a great chapel speaker or that I had a "good spirit" when I preached, but because it was time to introduce the speaker.

I am not sure what I preached that morning, but I do believe I better understood what Saint Paul meant in II Timothy 4:2a,

"Preach the word; be instant in season, out of season." That morning I was instant "out of season." It was anything but an ideal situation leading up to my entering the pulpit to preach to the student body that memorable Monday morning.

Looking back over more than forty years of preaching the gospel, I am thankful for that experience because I have often entered the pulpit with less than ideal circumstances prior to preaching. On one occasion years later I rode a train for twenty-one hours, and then, with only a couple hours break, I preached the opening service of a revival. On other occasions I have gone into the sanctuary while the congregation was singing and walked straight to the platform to preach. Several months ago after arriving during the song service, I was asked from the pulpit if I would preach, and, yes, I got out of my seat, went to the pulpit, and shared the precious Word of God.

I will never forget that chapel service when everything went wrong before the service, but I still trusted God, and He helped me preach even if it was "out of season." Had I waited for perfect conditions to prevail before I consented to preach, I fear I would not have preached many times.

Story 38

Preaching During My Senior Year

Frequently during my senior year of college, I preached somewhere on Sunday. It is amazing to read notes which I made at that time like this one: "Preached at the Sny Church of God Church near Louisiana, Missouri. Put $5.45 worth of gas in my car to go there and filled it up for $4.00 upon my return to Overland Park. I received $35.00 for preaching."

I received several calls to fill the pulpit for pastors who were away. I filled in for Herbert Lawson at the Church of God (Holiness) Church in Belton, Missouri, a suburb of Kansas City. I also preached at the Church of God (Holiness) Church in Kansas City North a couple of Sundays during their time of transition between pastors.

A highlight of my senior year was to be invited to preach a weekend revival at the Church of God (Holiness) Church in Olathe, Kansas. Burl McClanahan was the pastor. You recall he was the dear saint who said, "Brother Steve, I appreciated the good spirit of your message this morning," when I preached so pitifully as a college freshman during a chapel service. During that revival Ralph Beckham, my former boss at the Johnson County Library, sang specials and played his guitar. It was not an outstanding revival with new people being converted, but it was a time of refreshing and renewing. The offering from the revival was enough for me to purchase the recently completed *Beacon Bible Commentary*. It proved to be a very helpful investment as I still am using that set of commentaries. I am thankful that the revival offering allowed me to make the purchase.

Helen and I traveled one weekend per month to Peoria where I preached at the Wesleyan Holiness Church. I appreciated the love and kindness those precious people showered upon us. I learned a great deal as a once-a-month pastor. One Sunday morning I asked if anyone had a special. Before I had the sentence completed, a man was walking to the front of the little basement church with his harmonica ready to play for us. He attempted to play "The Beautiful Garden of Prayer." I learned that the dear man had never been to the church previously and was unknown to anyone in the church. Well, we had a special that Sunday morning, but I learned from then on that I was not going to open the service for just anyone to take part.

I went to Bible school to prepare for the ministry, and God helped me in many wonderful ways. I did make one profound discovery while at KCCBS—a true minister always is preparing for the ministry. He spends time earnestly praying and carefully studying for his sermon. His preparation is ongoing. The Apostle Paul wrote to Timothy, his son in the faith, and said, "Study to shew thyself approved unto God, a workman that needeth not to be ashamed, rightly dividing the word of truth" (II Timothy 2:15). An older minister was asked what he was doing, and his reply was, "I am studying for the ministry." After decades of preaching sermons and pastoring churches, he realized that he continually needed to study and prepare for the most important business in the world, preaching the Word of God.

Story 39

Car Number Three

My first car was a black 1953 Packard. I drove it for four months and sold it to Clifford Phillips for $65.00 before I went to Bible school. My second car was a white 1962 Ford Fairlane 500. I drove my Ford for two and a half years, and for a number of months, I wanted to upgrade but nothing developed. I even looked at a 1967 Plymouth Fury III in Quincy one weekend while I was in Illinois, but the price was more than I wanted to pay. A few days later my dad bought the car for himself. Often I am ready to trade cars several months before the Lord is ready for me to trade.

I always enjoyed looking at the classified ads in the newspaper, and I was looking for a deal on a low-mileage, clean car that would last a long time for a preacher. I wanted to have a dependable car when I graduated that was paid for and suitable for us.

Then it happened that I saw the ad for which I had been searching: a 1966 Plymouth Fury II, two-door, six-cylinder, with 29,000 actual miles for $650.00. I wrote down the phone number, called about it, and arranged for Helen to go with me to see it. When we arrived, I was impressed. It was white and very clean. I test-drove it and felt at peace. When I got back from driving it, the owner wanted an answer as a party was there to test-drive it if I did not want the car. I told her I would have to pray about it and call her. I prayed, "Lord, if you want us to have this car, cause the people driving it not to take it." God heard my prayer, and Helen and I agreed to buy it. My brother Rodney bought the Ford Fairlane 500 which allowed us to pay cash for the Plymouth. I knew that as a minister, I would not have a great deal of money, so I did not want to be making car payments. The car was truly a plain model without even a radio. God blessed it, and we drove that car 99,000 miles. Praise the Lord!

The Bible says in Proverbs 22:7b, "The borrower is servant to the lender." I did not want to be the servant of the lender. I wanted to be the servant of the Lord Jesus Christ. In Romans 13:8 we read,

"Owe no man any thing, but to love one another: for he that loveth another hath fulfilled the law." Long before Dave Ramsey ever started Financial Peace University, I found peace by not going into debt. That practice has allowed me the liberty to follow freely the leadership of the Holy Spirit that indebtedness would never have permitted.

Wynn Lindahl in foreground and me with my 1966 Plymouth Fury II

Story 40

Graduation at Last

At last, June 2, 1971, arrived. All the required courses had been completed. The reading assignments, the term papers, the oral reports, the tests, and a hundred and one other requirements were now history. My school bill was paid. Today was the long-awaited graduation day!

My parents traveled to Overland Park to be present for that milestone in their firstborn son's life. I am sure they hardly could believe it was happening; they were not alone, and neither could I.

Steve and Helen after his baccalaureate service. Their third-floor apartment is in the background.

Graduation evening was truly a time of pomp and circumstance. In fact, there were three graduations that evening, including eighth grade, high school, and college. On that night of nights, the all-important one to me was college graduation. That night I was to receive a Bachelor of Arts degree in Social Studies with a minor in Religion.

Wearing my long black graduation gown and mortarboard, I walked through flower-covered archways to the college graduates' section. It did not seem possible that I had reached the goal. I had said it many times, "He that endureth unto the end, the same shall be graduated." Now it was about to happen. Thanks be to Jesus!

During that graduation ceremony, an award was to be given for the first time. Esther Adams, wife of Leroy S. Adams, Sr., had passed to her eternal reward on March 30, 1971. That dear holiness saint had been faithful until death and had received the crown of life. A special award, the Esther Adams Award, was established in her honor. That award was to be presented to the outstanding ministerial or missionary student. I had seen Carl Myers working on the trophy made in the shape of a cross. Like everything Carl did, it was prepared beautifully.

Esther Adams, in whose honor a special award was established

I was not expecting to be called to the platform to receive the trophy. It was a shock of shocks when Professor Omar Lee, the Ministerial Department Head, called for Steve Manley to come forward. A farm boy from Fishhook became the first student to receive the Esther Adams Award. Wow! I could not believe it. To God be all the glory for making it possible!

As the graduates exited the auditorium, I found it easy to smile with a diploma in one hand and a large metal cross representing the Esther Adams Award in the other hand. One fellow commented that as I marched down the aisle that night in my black robe with the large cross in my hand, I reminded him of Martin Luther. No

Receiving the Esther Adams Award. Professor Omar Lee standing on the left and Dr. Burl McClanahan sitting on the right.

doubt my size and the robe were the major comparisons. The cross trophy remained at KCCBS and names were added to mine in future years. I received a small plaque to keep.

After the photographs were taken in and around the auditorium, we removed our hot gowns and mortarboards and changed into street clothes. My brother-in-law Doug Lyon and I graduated together that night and had a combined party at the school dining hall with our families. It certainly was a blessed evening and a milestone worth struggling to obtain.

Bob and Marge Hodges and their six children came all the way from Merrill, Michigan, for Doug and my graduation. On their way to KCCBS, a semi-truck driver fell asleep and drove into their pop-up camper. Although the camper was destroyed, no one was injured, and their station wagon was not damaged. We thank God for His mercy just before graduation.

The graduation motto was taken

Doug and Becky Lyon and Helen and me at the graduation party

from part of I Corinthians 14:12, "Seek that ye may excel." Those are indeed challenging words for every Christian. The Apostle Paul stressed that believers should excel in edifying the Church of Jesus Christ. As a college graduate it was my desire to excel for the glory of God.

The following article, written by President Dale M. Yocum, appeared in the *Church Herald and Holiness Banner*, the official paper of the Church of God (Holiness).

THE PRODUCT of KCCBS

Every factory has its produce, which goes out as an advertisement of the institution which produced it. The product may be a new automobile, a felt hat, or a pair of leather shoes. The product is the end for which the institution exists. Our Bible schools exist for a a similar purpose: to yield a product. Our production is not in terms of manufactured goods, however, but in lives prepared to go forth bearing the image of Christ.

It is always a joy to approach the end of a school term and look upon the young lives that have been indoctrinated in Biblical truth and conformed to the image of the Master. You will see in the accompanying picture one young couple that will soon be leaving KCCBS to enter the ministry of the Gospel. Steve and Helen Manley were unacquainted until they enrolled at KCCBS. Here, they met; here they studied; from here they will be going out joined together as a team of devoted, sanctified messengers for Christ. We deeply appreciate Steve and Helen. They have been consistent, spiritual, modest, and true to God's best. We want our people to know them and pray for them as they leave this sacred campus to take up their post in the Lord's service. They are planning, upon Steve's graduation, to enter upon a pastorate in Illinois. Helen has been working faithfully in the school business office. We will miss both of them, but will be happy to have them in the harvest field, as products of God's grace and KCCBS.

Dale M. Yocum, president.

(Used by permission of *Church Herald and Holiness Banner*.)

For a college freshman who came to Bible school with limited potential, God helped him through four years of college and allowed him to graduate from Kansas City College and Bible School. All glory goes to the Lord Jesus Christ who made it possible that a farm boy from Fishhook would graduate and be bestowed with such honor.

Story 41

Leaving Kansas for Our First Pastorate

After my graduation from Kansas City College and Bible School, we remained on campus until the general camp of the Church of God (Holiness) was over. Helen worked in the business office and was needed until after camp.

We rented the smallest box truck that Penske Truck Rental had available and prepared to move to Peoria. The day we loaded the truck, Silas McGhee came by and made a profound prophecy. He said, "Brother Steve, you will never move again in a truck this small." My wife and I only had a hide-a-bed, a green swivel rocker, a wooden rocking chair, a bedstead and open springs but no mattress, a chest of drawers, a stereo system, a desk and chair, a small cedar chest, a large lamp, a bookcase and some books, and our clothes. The truck certainly was loaded lightly.

Helen and I went to the home of Reverend and Mrs. R.E. Carroll for a brunch in their backyard the morning we departed from KCCBS. It was a special time before leaving the big city. Helen drove our Plymouth, and I drove the truck. We traveled to Fishhook and

Parsonage at 514 East Washington Street

108

spent the night with my parents. My Great-Uncle John Lane gave us a refrigerator that we added to our things in the rental truck. The next afternoon we traveled about two hours to 514 East Washington Street, East Peoria, Illinois, our parsonage home address.

In the evening men from the church helped us unload the truck. A couple from the church gave us a bedroom suite—bedstead, open springs, two mattresses, and a vanity. KY Oldham gave us a kitchen table and four chairs. The church gave us a gas range and the previous renter left two chairs in the living room. Within a few hours the Lord graciously provided the needed furnishings for our two-bedroom parsonage home.

The Bible says in Philippians 4:19, "But my God shall supply all your need according to his riches in glory by Christ Jesus." He did just that. Our kitchen had a gas stove, refrigerator, and a small table. The master bedroom had a full-size bed, vanity, and dresser. After sleeping on a hide-a-bed for two years, it was wonderful to have a bed that did not need to be folded up each day. The guest room had a double bed. The living room had the hide-a-bed couch, a large lamp, a glass-topped table, end tables, a coffee table, a stereo, a green swivel chair, and two small chairs. The dining room had the table and chairs, bookcase, and rocking chair. Soon a wringer washing machine was given to us, and we were washing our clothes the old-fashion way.

Granted, we were not going to be featured in *Better Homes and Gardens* magazine, but we had all that we needed plus the contentment that only Jesus gives. The Bible says in Hebrews 13:5, "Let your conversation be without covetousness; and be content with such things as ye have: for he hath said, I will never leave thee, nor forsake thee." Helen and I were truly content with such things as the Lord had provided.

The church was small, and my salary was $50.00 per week. The church paid the rent on the parsonage of $125.00 per month plus the utilities. We felt the Lord wanted us to live by faith and trust Him to meet our every need so that I could give myself to the ministry. Hebrews 13:6 says, "So that we may boldly say, The Lord is my helper, and I will not fear what man shall do unto me." Truly the Lord was our helper as we assumed the role of pastor of the Wesleyan Holiness Church of Peoria.

Peoria parishioners

Terry and Alberta Berry

Robert, Frances, and Marie Ritthaler

Glen, Jeff, and Pat Dyer

Abbie, Deanna,
Jeanene, and Bob
Shoesmith

Melba and Francis Lee

Ruth Howard and
granddaughter

Dorothy Berry

Story 42

Preacher, Painter, and Paper Hanger

It was a blessing to preach the Word of God twice on Sunday and lead the Wednesday evening prayer meeting. Soon I was calling on patients in the local hospitals and visiting church members in their homes. Two ladies were always making new contacts for the church. Sometimes the addresses and directions to those homes were challenging. Once I was told to call on a lady in the white house on Main Street. Sad to say I never found that lady because of the many white houses. I was delighted to at last be in full-time Christian service.

It, no doubt, took an abundance of grace to put up with me as I started pastoring, but the dear people had been without a resident pastor for over nine months. When I arrived, they were happy to have a regular preacher and treated my wife and me like royalty. It was noteworthy that I followed Reverend H.L. Fuller in that pastorate. I had spent the weekend in the Fuller home during a weekend meeting in November of 1968 when Grace Fuller introduced me to creamed eggs for breakfast.

The Peoria Wesleyan Holiness congregation worshipped at 1926 Lincoln Avenue in a basement building. The church was built

The front of the church at 1926 Lincoln Avenue

with a stucco front that faced the street. As you entered the building, there were rest rooms on either side of the vestibule and a stairway leading to the basement. The roof was flat and covered with rolled roofing and coated with tar to keep out the water. Sad to say, after a few years flat roofs tend to leak; our church roof was no exception. It leaked before I came, and the ceiling tiles had many ugly brown spots. Soon we were painting the tiles and covering those brown spots. It was a big improvement. I regularly had to put tar on the roof to keep that flat roof from leaking.

The stucco exterior was in need of paint, but the church budget would not budge enough to buy paint to do the job. Reverend and Mrs. C. Dean Grant pastored the Church of God (Holiness) Church in neighboring Bellevue, Illinois, and gave us a recipe for whitewashing the stucco. We bought some lime at the hardware store, added buttermilk and a few other things, and used it to brighten up the stucco. Within a few hours the outside of the church looked much cleaner and brighter.

The parsonage was in great need of fresh wallpaper. The house was owned by the Free Methodist Church, and the congregation was willing to provide the wallpaper if we were willing to hang it. As a boy, I had watched my mother and Aunt Cleo hang wallpaper in our old farm house. I remembered it was a big job and required some special tools. There was a layman in the Church of God (Holiness) Church by the name of Lester Jones who had all the necessary tools. Although he was an elderly man, he with his pastor, C. Dean Grant and his wife, Wilma, and I were willing to attempt the wallpapering task. It was only a two-bedroom house, but by the time we were through with the task, it seemed like a palace in size. It greatly improved the looks of the house, and we sincerely appreciated the labors of Lester and the Grants.

A few days after the wallpapering job was completed, Lester could not find his putty knife. He looked everywhere he could think of and knew he used it when doing the wallpapering. He told his pastor about it, and we looked diligently for the lost putty knife. It was decided that I would purchase a new putty knife for Lester because, apparently, it was lost during the wallpapering job.

I went to the local hardware store and purchased the best one they had in the one-inch style like the one that was missing. Lester was happy, I was happy, and all was well. Then one day while working in his shop, Lester moved something and found his long-lost putty knife. He returned the new one that I had purchased, and I got to keep the best putty knife the hardware store carried for my personal use. I used that putty knife for nearly forty years until one day I broke the blade while prying with it. It certainly paid to restore with the best available.

The Bible teaches us to restore in Deuteronomy 22:1-2: "Thou shalt not see thy brother's ox or his sheep go astray, and hide thyself from them: thou shalt in any case bring them again unto thy brother. And if thy brother be not nigh unto thee, or if thou know him not, then thou shalt bring it unto thine own house, and it shall be with thee until thy brother seek after it, and thou shalt restore it to him again."

Story 43

"You Don't Have Enough Religion"

The morning after I gave my heart to Jesus Christ, a friend approached me before classes at our high school and said, "Steve, I heard you got religion last night." I hardly knew how to respond to that remark but affirmed that it was true. Religion was not really what I needed; I had lots of that before I got saved. What I needed was salvation. Thankfully, the Lord Jesus Christ saved me and gave me the best religion on earth.

When I was a student at KCCBS, I was encouraged to pursue a Bachelor of Arts degree, and on June 2, 1971, that degree was conferred upon me. After I joined the Wesleyan Holiness Association of Churches, the Ministerial Studies Committee looked over my transcript and concluded, "You don't have enough religion for ordination." What it meant was that although I had met the requirements for a Bachelor of Arts degree, I had not taken enough theology classes and other religious and ministerial courses to become an ordained minister in the Wesleyan Holiness Association of Churches. Therefore, I needed to take several subjects from their home-study course for ministers to meet the requirements of ordination. Although I was disappointed, I was willing to do what was required to become an ordained elder in the Association.

Soon I was reading books, taking tests, and fulfilling the prescribed course of studies to become ordained. At times is seemed like much extra work, but I came to realize that the Ministerial Studies Committee was right. I had some large gaps in my ministerial studies and profited greatly from the extra education. Some of the material that I was required to study was useful in preparing for the church services. I combined sermon preparation and my ministerial studies and greatly benefited from it. Hopefully, the church gained as many spiritual benefits as their pastor. I am thankful for the many authors that I met during that course of study: Orton Wiley, A.B. Simpson, Glenn Griffith, Samuel Logan

Brengle, Rees Howells, G.D. Watson and others. I have read and reread some of those books many times.

Years later when a young preacher was not happy about the requirements the Ministerial Studies Committee told him he needed to pursue, I could tell the dear fellow, "I had to do it, too. It will be good for you. It helped me a great deal."

Once I had completed the home-study course, I realized that with my Bachelor of Arts degree, I had met nearly all the requirements for a Bachelor of Arts degree in Missions from KCCBS. I contacted the college and was able to take some additional courses by correspondence, and by using the credits from the home-study course, I was able to receive a second degree on May 30, 1975. That degree was a Bachelor of Arts in Missions with a major in Religion and a minor in Social Studies.

I learned in my first pastorate that the pastor needs to be a life-long student. One day I met another minister at the hospital. He was calling on a member of his church, and I was calling on a member from my church. He had a book in his hand and was reading while waiting for the member to get out of surgery. That man told me it was his goal to read a new book or booklet every week. That is a noble goal. It was little wonder that he was pastoring one of the largest churches in his conference at that time.

When the gospel came to Berea, those believers became serious students of the Word of God. The Bible says in Acts 17:11, "These were more noble than those in Thessalonica, in that they received the word with all readiness of mind, and searched the scriptures daily, whether those things were so." In II Timothy 3:16-17 we read: "All scripture is given by inspiration of God, and is profitable for doctrine, for reproof, for correction, for instruction in righteousness: That the man of God may be perfect, throughly furnished unto all good works." I learned that I never could have too much knowledge of the Word of God and have striven to be a student of God's Holy Word.

Story 44

Attending a Camp Meeting and a Ministerial

When a minister is serving as the pastor of a church, he normally is responsible for several services per week. It is common for the pastor to preach two times on Sunday and conduct the midweek prayer meeting. Then if you add a funeral here and there with a wedding or two, the preacher speaks frequently. As the months roll by, the minister longs to hear someone else preach. Early in my ministry I found great spiritual benefits in attending our district camp meetings. Those days set aside for spiritual renewal and revival were like an oasis in the desert. The preaching of others was helpful to my soul, and I sincerely appreciated those times.

In August 1971, the general camp of the Wesleyan Holiness Association of Churches was held at West Milton, Ohio. It was my first time to attend our general camp, so I was all eyes and ears. The campground was lovely with many trees and well-kept cottages. My wife and I pitched our tent for our lodging during the camp. O.L. Fay was the camp evangelist, Glenn Griffith was the general superintendent, and Leroy Adams, Sr. was in charge of the music and orchestra. It was good to see my teacher again. I got one of his $1.00 haircuts during the camp meeting. I thoroughly enjoyed the services.

The business sessions of a general conference were a new experience for me, but I listened and learned. The Sunday afternoon ordination service was special as fifteen ministers were ordained into the ministry that day. The following were ordained: Howard Ayars, Darrell Bowden, James Davis, James Hayden, Michael Neese, James Patterson, Keith Schwanz, Archie B. Atwell, David Gardner, Gerald Mullen, Harley Newman, Hollis Robinson, Jr., Phillip Thompson, Steven E. Hight, and Russell Ulrich, Jr.

A joint ministerial was held in Canton, Ohio, in October 1971. Leaders and ministers from the God's Missionary Church, Midwest Pilgrim Holiness Church, New York Pilgrim Holiness Church, and Wesleyan Holiness Association of Churches came together for a

116

three-day convention. The little church in Peoria wanted their pastor and his wife to attend those meetings. An offering of $75.00 was given to the Manleys to help make that possible.

We packed the Plymouth and headed to Columbus, Ohio, where we spent the night with our good friends from Bible school, Tom and Sherry Peak. Tom was pastoring the Allegheny Wesleyan

Tom and Sherry Peak in Columbus, OH

Methodist Church there. It was great to be with the Peaks again. We both had small home-mission type churches. The Peaks were sacrificing but happy in the service of the King. I recall they did not have a cook stove, but she fixed a good meal using an electric skillet and a crock pot. When it was time for ice cream, Sherry opened the half-gallon container from the bottom, and thus it looked like it was full. Tom spoke up and told her she had opened the wrong end. Poor Sherry, she had already used part of the carton of ice cream but did not want us to know they were short on ice cream. Many of us on our first pastorates did similar things so people would not know just how low supplies were in the parsonage.

Tuesday found us saying good-bye to the Peaks and pointing the Plymouth toward Canton. As we traveled, people in a yellow Volkswagen passed us and then slowed down, and I passed them. They were an older holiness couple, and they waved and followed us all the way to Canton. When I stopped at a gas station to ask for directions to the Crystal Park Wesleyan Church, they pulled in behind us and asked if we were going to the holiness convention. We told them we were, and after getting directions, they followed us to the church.

Finding a motel was not easy for a farm boy from Fishhook with only a shoestring budget. We found an old hotel in downtown Canton that provided us a room for three nights for $16.64. It was not anything about which to brag, and the sheets had patches on them, but we stayed there, and God watched over the drunks and us. Thankfully, the place did not burn down while we were there. A new donut shop had opened near the church, and it was having a special on donuts for $.99 per dozen. Several of us who attended the convention ate donuts for breakfast.

One evening we went to McDonald's and ate in our car. We were parked next to Reverend and Mrs. Andrew J. Whitney, the president and his wife of the New York Pilgrim Holiness Church. We had no idea we would be able to eat with such a distinguished ministerial couple during the convention and at such a world-renowned restaurant.

I bought my first tank of unleaded gasoline in Canton. The change from leaded to unleaded gas was just taking place. We traveled about 900 miles round-trip and spent a total of $21.26 for gas. The most costly fill-up was $7.90.

The services were outstanding, and the preaching by James Southerland, Paul Miller, Glenn Griffith, and others was tremendous. The Crystal Park Wesleyan Church did a fine job of hosting the convention, and their people certainly took their liberty in praising the Lord during the night services. The papers presented during the day sessions by various ministers were thought provoking and challenging.

The October weather was lovely, and the trees were exceedingly beautiful. I remarked to my wife both going to and coming from the convention that it was like we were driving through a fall picture

Front row: Andrew J. Whitney, James Southerland, Paul Martin, Glenn Griffith. Back row: O.L. Fay, Allen Russell, L. Wayne States

on a calendar. It was a never-to-be-forgotten ministerial convention, and I met ministers and laymen whose friendships I have cherished ever since. Psalm 133:1 says, "Behold, how good and how pleasant it is for brethren to dwell together in unity!" It was great to attend the ministerial in Canton.

Story 45

His Name Is on the Prayer List

One Sunday night when I was in a room praying before the service started, I heard a new voice in the sanctuary. It was a man's voice, and that church did not have an abundance of men, so I wondered who could be visiting our service. When I came from the room, my eyes fell upon an older, bald-headed man in the rear of the church. I conducted the service, preached my message, and then slipped to the back of the church during the closing prayer. As I greeted the stranger, he introduced himself. "My name is Ed Berry. The woods is full of them," meaning that there were many Berrys—just like many berries in the woods. His sense of humor made me smile, but his name made me rejoice. Ed went on to say, "I am just an old backslider."

I had asked the church for the names of people they wanted to see saved, and we Christians were praying for those on that prayer list. When the man gave me his name, Ed Berry, I recognized him as one of those spiritually needy individuals on the church prayer list. Not long after appearing in the Sunday night service, Ed gave his heart to the Lord Jesus Christ in the home of Robert and Deanna Shoesmith.

Ed came to the fall revival in November of 1971 when Larry Warren was the evangelist. One night Robert Shoesmith asked me to go with him to get Ed for the revival service. Ed wanted to go to the A & P grocery store before coming to church. In his loud commanding voice, he asked to speak to the manager of the store. When he was not available, Ed openly confessed to the assistant manager that he had pilfered some things from that store and wanted to pay for the stolen items. The assistant manager said, "You want to pay me for things you stole and did not get caught?" Ed replied, "Yes, I got saved, and I want to make it right." Again the assistant manager said, "You want to pay me for things you took and never got caught?" Ed said, "That is right." The assistant manager said he did not want the money. Ed replied, "Our church is in revival. May I put the money in the offering?" He agreed for him to do so. The poor fellow was dumbfounded to have someone pay for things he had stolen and did not get caught. Ed made other restitutions when I was with him, one for not paying a hospital bill and another for using pieces of metal in a pool table instead of quarters.

Ed Berry frequently testified in the revival services to the saving grace of the Lord Jesus. His changed life was manifested by his willingness to make his wrongs right and walk in the light. Thus he grew in the grace and knowledge of the Lord Jesus Christ.

Many years have passed since the name of Ed Berry, a seventy-year-old backslider, appeared on the church prayer list in Peoria. Eventually, he had a stroke and soon thereafter passed from this life into eternity. Thankfully, the church prayed for him while he was in the land of the living. It is now too late to pray for the spiritual needs of Ed Berry.

Revelation 22:11 says, "He that is unjust, let him be unjust still: and he which is filthy, let him be filthy still: and he that is righteous, let him be righteous still: and he that is holy, let him be holy still." There is a great need for the people of God to unite in prayer for the conversion of sinners and the restoration of backsliders. The Apostle Paul believed in praying seriously for those who were without Christ. Please read his words in Galatians 4:19, "My little children, of whom I travail in birth again until Christ be formed in you." Paul prayed seriously and fervently until Christ was formed in the heart of the person for whom he prayed.

Reverend C.L. Henbest, a Church of the Nazarene evangelist, was called to a church that had a prayer list, and prior to his arrival had prayed through that one hundred people would be saved in the revival meeting. God moved in a mighty way in answer to prayer, and one hundred people whose names were on the list were saved in the revival in spite of a large snowstorm.

Jesus said in Matthew 18:19, "That if two of you shall agree on earth as touching any thing that they shall ask, it shall be done for them of my Father which is in heaven." The Holy Spirit inspired Peter to write II Peter 3:9, "The Lord is not slack concerning his promise, as some men count slackness; but is longsuffering to us-ward, not willing that any should perish, but that all should come to repentance." Do you have a list of sinners and backsliders for whom you are praying regularly? Do you agree with others for the conversion of those on a mutual prayer list? There is a great need today for united prayer for sinners and backsliders.

Story 46

A Bunch of Beans and a Brand-New Baby

The Lord provided for our needs in various ways during our years in Peoria. Francis Lee and Robert Ritthaler, two men in the church, loved to do gardening in the summer. Those dear men shared their harvest with the pastor and his wife. We enjoyed fresh vegetables and canned them, too. On July 18, I picked a bunch of green beans, and Helen canned twelve quarts and five pints of beans. That evening we went to the Methodist Hospital and attended a class for soon-to-be parents. On the way home from the hospital, my wife jokingly said, "Do you want to take me back to the hospital tonight?" I assured her that if she needed to go to the hospital that night, I would be happy to take her.

Very early the next morning Helen awakened with contractions. Because her due date was eight days away, she did not have a bag packed to take to the hospital. She awakened me and prepared her bag for the hospital. I dressed, shaved, and periodically timed the contractions. We decided this was the real thing. In the inky early morning darkness, we returned to the Methodist Hospital.

Brenda and her father in the hospital

My wife encouraged me to drive faster after we crossed the Illinois River. She really wanted to get to the hospital. It was a good thing we did not tarry much longer because we were only in the hospital fifty-eight minutes before Brenda Jean joined our family on July 19, 1972. She tipped the scales at 8 pounds and 2 ounces and was 20 inches long. Many mothers have envied my wife's quick delivery, but because of the rapid progress of the birthing process, her blood pressure soared. Thankfully, all went well for mother and daughter along with dear old Dad.

Brenda was born on Wednesday morning. When I called Francis and Melba Lee to announce Brenda's birth, I asked him to lead the prayer meeting service that evening.

We were delighted to have Brenda join our family. We really had not expected our baby to be a redhead, but because Helen's paternal grandfather was a redhead and some of Brenda's cousins have red hair, we should have considered the possibility. Aside from being a beautiful baby, that red hair generated a number of comments, even from total strangers.

Helen had been paying the doctor's fee when she went for her checkups, and it was almost paid at the time of Brenda's birth. Being on a small salary of $60.00 per week, it made the hospital bill of $409.59 look very large to us. Thankfully, the hospital gave us a 12½ percent ministerial discount. The Lord encouraged our faith as we prayed, and by the time the bill was due, we were able to pay it in full. To God be all the glory and praise!

Brenda was the first grandchild for my parents. When my mother called Dad at the Gardner Denver plant in Quincy, it was announced over the public-address system that Harry Manley was a new grandfather and that the mother and daughter were doing fine. My parents and my two brothers, Rodney and Len, came to visit us on the weekend, especially to see Brenda.

Brenda at five days with her Manley grandparents

Suddenly we were no longer just a couple; now we were a family! Psalm 127:3 reads, "Lo, children are an heritage of the LORD: and the fruit of the womb is his reward." The blessing of fatherhood also brought with it many challenges and responsibilities. The sobering words of Ephesians 6:4 took on new meaning to me as I read, "And, ye fathers, provoke not your children to

Brenda and her great-grandparents
Cora and Cale Manley

wrath: but bring them up in the nurture and admonition of the Lord." Parenting certainly was a new challenge for a young pastor.

Brenda with her first Christmas doll

Story 47

A Bad Accident

God had blessed my wife and me with a lovely little redheaded daughter, Brenda Jean. Things were going well for my wife and our new daughter. We were happy parents.

It seems that after an outstanding blessing there is often a very difficult circumstance that comes our way. Elijah had a great victory on Mount Carmel, and shortly thereafter the queen wanted him dead. He found himself in deep depression under a juniper tree, wishing he could die. Helen and Brenda were in the hospital on the morning of July 20. I went to the church and mowed the grass. After mowing I loaded the Lawn Boy mower into the trunk of our Plymouth and headed down Lincoln Avenue to our home in East Peoria. I had traveled only a few blocks when a two-year-old boy ran into the street right in front of my car. He was hit by the front fender and thrown several feet. I quickly stopped and saw the little fellow on the ground. I rushed into a bar and had the bartender call an ambulance. Later I learned that Michael Evans and his older brother had gone into that bar and purchased pop and potato chips for their breakfast. Young Michael came into the street and was hit by my Plymouth. It was a horrible feeling to see that little boy lying in the street with a serious head injury, and I felt completely helpless. Soon the ambulance took him to the Methodist Hospital, the hospital where my wife and newborn baby were patients.

I prayed for Michael's family many times and for his complete restoration. I frequently went to our garage and prayed exclusively for him. Finally, in December of 1972, the angels came and took him into the presence of Jesus. He had never regained consciousness since the accident in July.

There were legal matters through which I had to go as a result of the accident. The hospital bills were beyond the limits of my insurance coverage. It was certainly not a pleasant time in the life of a young preacher. Thankfully, my car insurance company worked through the many challenges that arose, and I faced neither legal nor financial problems as a result of that horrible accident. As difficult as the whole ordeal was, I have been able to share my story with others who found themselves involved in accidents and situations that were very hard to face.

The Bible says in I Corinthians 10:13, "There hath no temptation taken you but such as is common to man: but God is faithful, who will not suffer you to be tempted above that ye are able; but will with the temptation also make a way to escape, that ye may be able to bear it." The passage in II Corinthians 1:3-4 says: "Blessed be God, even the Father of our Lord Jesus Christ, the Father of mercies, and the God of all comfort; Who comforteth us in all our tribulation, that we may be able to comfort them which are in any trouble, by the comfort wherewith we ourselves are comforted of God." It was certainly a difficult time in my life, but I found Jesus was there during the times when I was tempted to question why God allowed the accident to happen.

Story 48

Evangelistic Faith Missions Missionaries

One of the blessings of pastoring the Peoria Wesleyan Holiness Church was the emphasis the church placed upon missions. The church had a monthly missions service and featured missionaries serving with Evangelistic Faith Missions. Letters from the missionaries were read, prayer requests were shared, and a monthly offering was taken. I never had attended a church that placed that much emphasis on missions, but I liked it very much.

Leroy S. Adams, Jr. and his wife, Myrtle, had been missionaries with Evangelistic Faith Missions in Africa. My wife and I came to know them when they were home on furlough and visited his parents while we were at KCCBS. In October of 1971, Leroy was in the Peoria area having services, and he stayed in our home for three nights. He went to different churches for those meetings. One of those services was at our church. Although the congregation was not large, the people were missions minded and were willing to move their midweek prayer meeting to a different night to have a missionary service. We enjoyed listening to Leroy play his trumpet and accordion at the same time. His stories from Ethiopia were exciting and enlightening.

Again in February of 1972, Leroy was in our area, and because he did not have any scheduled services, he consented to have impromptu services at our church on February 11, 12, and 13. Our people were delighted to hear him again. He remarked that he enjoyed eating simple foods and that chili was a real treat. We were thankful to have him as a guest in our humble home.

I had never met Faith Hemmeter until Easter time in 1972. Her parents were pastoring in Canton, Illinois, and they brought her to our home on Saturday evening. We had a sunrise service plus a special Easter foreign missions service with Faith speaking. My wife had known the Hemmeter family when they lived in Michigan, and Walter Hemmeter was one of her Bible school teachers. The

Faith Hemmeter in front of the Lincoln Avenue Church
on Easter morning

Hemmeters invited us to their parsonage home, so we joined them and their two children, Faith and John, for Easter Sunday dinner.

It was a blessing to meet and entertain EFM missionaries in our church and in our home. Over the four years we pastored in the Peoria area, we were privileged to have Leroy Adams, Jr., Faith Hemmeter, Keith Schwanz, Leonard Sankey, Juddie Peyton, and Gary Gellerman in our church and home.

Juddie Peyton was a guest in our home for a weekend when he was checking about putting the radio ministry of Evangelistic Faith Missions on the local station WPEO. The holiness ministerial association of that area had requested that that be done, and for more than thirty-five years, the Missionary and Evangelistic Broadcast was aired over that station.

The Bible says in Hebrews 13:1-2: "Let brotherly love continue. Be not forgetful to entertain strangers: for thereby some have entertained angels unawares." Again in I Peter 4:9 the Bible says, "Use hospitality one to another without grudging."

Story 49

Conducting Funerals

As a minister of the gospel, at times I was asked to officiate at funerals. One of our church members had a sister who was in the hospital. I called on her on several occasions but was unable to be of great help to her by either praying for her healing or receiving Jesus Christ as her personal Savior. The family had no church affiliation, and when she died, I was asked to officiate at the funeral.

It was my first funeral. I was rather nervous, but God helped me to minister to the living. I spoke from the words of David in I Samuel 20:3c where he said, "There is but a step between me and death." It was a simple funeral, and soon the dear lady was laid to rest. It was so sad to officiate at the funeral of one who "having no hope, and without God in the world" slipped out of this life to face the Judge of the Universe.

The second funeral at which I officiated was that of Elsie Balzer, my maternal grandmother, on September 26, 1972. Grandma Balzer was a sincere Christian. Once when I visited her after my own conversion to Christ, she answered the door on that Sunday afternoon with her Bible in her hand. Her circle in life was rather small. She was a farmer's wife with the continuous care of her epileptic son, Lilburn. Much of her time was spent caring for her family, gardening, and canning until her beloved husband, George, passed away. Lilburn was then institutionalized, and she sold the farm and moved to Liberty, Illinois.

During the last few years of Grandma's life, she was in a nursing home in Mt. Sterling, Illinois. The family asked me to officiate at the funeral which took place in the United Methodist Church in Kingston, Illinois. Donna Kistner sang at the service. God helped me to preach in a small country church filled with family and friends, and there were people present to whom I never preached before or since. Some men had to stand in the back of the church because of the lack of seating. Revelation 20:5-6 says: "But the rest of the dead lived not again until the thousand years were finished.

This is the first resurrection. Blessed and holy is he that hath part in the first resurrection: on such the second death hath no power, but they shall be priests of God and of Christ, and shall reign with him a thousand years." I hope to see Grandma Balzer in heaven.

The third funeral I conducted was that of Myrtle Sill. Some of the people in our church had a burden for Myrtle's spiritual condition, and we had a cottage prayer meeting in her home. She was 89 years of age at that time, and as we sang "Pass Me Not," she began to weep. We prayed with her, and I believe Jesus saved her. Some time passed, and when she died, I was asked to officiate at the funeral. I do not know of a family that took the loss of their mother any harder than the Sill family. The children were older and had their mother for so long that they had difficulty handling the loss.

My fourth funeral was that of Ella Lee. She was a Christian woman and a member of the Wesleyan Holiness Church that I was pastoring. She was very dear to my wife and me. Although she was not a woman of wealth, she sought ways to be helpful to us. Often gifts of food were received from that thoughtful saint.

Ella Lee

One time when Ella had a heart attack, her heart had to be shocked three times to revive her. It did not look like she would recover, but God allowed her to live and be with us a little longer. She told me: "Brother Manley, tell the people to do their praying before they get sick and go to the hospital. When I was in that Cardiac Care Unit, I was too sick to pray. I could not have gotten saved if I had wanted to." That is very good advice for those who are neglecting their soul's salvation. Eventually, Ella Lee's body wore out, and she went to be with the Lord. The funeral was at the Sunnyland Wesleyan Holiness Church. By the grace of God, I expect to see Ella Lee in heaven.

The Bible says in Hebrews 9:27-28: "And as it is appointed unto men once to die, but after this the judgment: So Christ was once offered to bear the sins of many; and unto them that look for him shall he appear the second time without sin unto salvation." Funerals are not pleasant times, but we all have an appointment with death. Many fail to prepare by repenting of their sins and becoming born-again Christians. Regardless, if you are prepared or not, you are going to die and then face the judgment.

Story 50

Glenn Griffith—An Outstanding Leader

Over the course of a lifetime, one meets only a few truly outstanding leaders. Glenn Griffith showed his leadership abilities during World War I on the battlefields of France. He served with distinction under enemy fire and earned great respect from the soldiers who were serving under his command.

After the War ended, he was converted and sanctified wholly in a camp meeting in Wichita, Kansas. In a short time he was the pastor of a church. Then he became a faithful holiness evangelist in the Church of the Nazarene and served as a district superintendent. His evangelistic fervor was superior to most.

Later he was the first General Superintendent of the Wesleyan Holiness Association of Churches. When I met him, he was an aging saint but still fervent in spirit and zealous for God. His messages were filled with the power of the Holy Spirit. He had a contagious way of causing you to want to be spiritual. He was truly a man full of the Holy Ghost and fire.

During my first year as pastor, Glenn Griffith came to Peoria for a weekend meeting on April 14-16, 1972. Phil and Mary Harris, one of my wife's sisters and her husband, came and visited us on Saturday. They loved and appreciated Brother Griffith. We had a good meeting, and God helped the church greatly during that visit by our beloved General Superintendent.

Glenn Griffith

The North Central District Camp and Conference was held near Groveland, Illinois,

June 13-17, 1973. Glenn Griffith served as the camp meeting evangelist and the presiding officer for the conference. The services were conducted at the Groveland Zion Evangelical Tabernacle grounds just east of Peoria. He stayed in our home during the meeting because it was a drive-in type of camp. What a blessing to have him with us for those few days.

The camp meeting at Groveland closed on Sunday, and on Monday Glenn Griffith flew to Kansas for the General Camp of the Wesleyan Holiness Association of Churches at Macksville. My wife and I loaded our Plymouth that same day with our clothing and supplies along with baby Brenda and traveled to Fishhook and spent the night with my parents. The next morning we stopped by KCCBS and visited friends and then continued on to Macksville. It was wheat harvest time in central Kansas, and we saw mile after mile of amber waves of grain. Gasoline crunch number one was in full swing, and we were allowed only a certain amount of gas at each filling station. We went to two gas stations to get enough gas for a fill-up. It was a long, hot trip as our old Plymouth did not have air-conditioning. We had a wonderful camp meeting with Glenn Griffith presiding over the camp and conference. George Straub was the evangelist, and Richard Beckham was the song evangelist. There were many times of great blessing and victory during the camp.

On June 21, 1973, the afternoon temperature was 105 degrees outside the tabernacle when I was ordained as an elder into the Wesleyan Holiness Association of Churches. Thankfully, the tabernacle was air conditioned. John Copeland, and Wesley and Fonetta Elliott, husband and wife, were ordained also in that service. Glenn Griffith gave the ordination message and prayed over each of us that hot June afternoon.

Glenn Griffith went to be with Jesus in January 1976. I was privileged to know him in the sunset years of his life and am very grateful.

The minister of the gospel has a high and holy calling. Ordination is the highest honor conferred upon a minister of the gospel. In Titus 1:5 we read, "For this cause left I thee in Crete, that thou shouldest set in order the things that are wanting, and ordain elders in every city, as I had appointed thee:"

The day of my ordination with L. Wayne States and Glenn Griffith

The Wesleyan Holiness Association of Churches set the standard high. When I was ordained they required me to complete their home-study course for ministers in addition to my Bachelor of Arts degree from KCCBS. I am a better man and a better minister for having been required to do so. That which costs nothing means nothing. My ordination means a great deal to me, and to have Glenn Griffith lay his hands upon me that hot afternoon in Kansas was indeed a special blessing.

Story 51

A Special Baptismal Service

One of the blessings I enjoy as a minister is officiating at a baptismal service. The Lord Jesus told his disciples in Matthew 28:19-20: "Go ye therefore, and teach all nations, baptizing them in the name of the Father, and of the Son, and of the Holy Ghost: Teaching them to observe all things whatsoever I have commanded you: and, lo, I am with you alway, even unto the end of the world. Amen."

It is wonderful to report the number of people who sought God at a public altar for spiritual needs such as salvation or entire sanctification. It is informative for the pastor to report the number of weddings and funerals at which he officiated during the conference year. I consider the number of people baptized during a certain period of time to be a good way of checking on the growth and success of a church.

After a person has repented of his sins and is walking in the light of God's Word, it is his privilege to receive water baptism. The rite of baptism is a testimony that the person is dead to the old life of sin and is resurrected to new life in Christ. It is very special when that service can be done in a public place like a river or lake so that the world can see it take place. I was baptized in McKee Creek at Wilson Ford. That Sunday afternoon service has been a significant spiritual landmark in my Christian life ever since it took place in the summer of 1966.

On April 10, 1973, I was privileged to baptize Robert, Deanna, and Debbie Shoesmith and Myra Gaddy. We did not have a good place for an outdoor baptismal service, and our church did not have a baptistery. The Church of the Bible Covenant had one and allowed us to use it. C.E. Fleshman was the pastor at the time of the baptismal service, and we had a joint service. It was a blessed time as the candidates gave their testimonies to their faith in the Lord Jesus Christ and were buried with Him in baptism.

I love what Romans 6:4 says, "Therefore we are buried with him by baptism into death: that like as Christ was raised up from the dead by the glory of the Father, even so we also should walk in newness of life." It is thrilling to know the resurrection power of the Lord Jesus Christ and testify to it by following Him in water baptism.

Story 52

Moving to Sunnyland

When I accepted the pastorate of the Peoria Wesleyan Holiness Church, the building left much to be desired. Being a basement church with a flat roof, we struggled with a leaky roof and some water seepage when it rained. I longed for a better building, but our congregation was neither large nor rich and moving would take God's direction and special help.

In the spring of 1973, we learned of a Church of the Nazarene building that was for sale east of Peoria in a subdivision called Sunnyland. The church building was not large, and the price was not extremely high. We began to consider prayerfully the possibili-

The Wesleyan Holiness Church at Sunnyland

ties of selling the Peoria church property and buying the Sunnyland church property. God worked out the many details, and on April 11, 1973, the Wesleyan Holiness Church voted to move. At the end of that month, the congregation voted to sell the church building at 1926 Lincoln Avenue. Our last service was on July 22, and our first service at the Sunnyland church was the following week. It was nice to have a better facility in which to worship the Lord.

L. Wayne States, the assistant general superintendent of the Wesleyan Holiness Association of Churches, came and dedicated the church on October 7. Arthur Thomas from Penns Creek, Pennsylvania, was Wayne States' traveling companion during that tour. It was good to have them as guests in our parsonage home.

I never will forget an event that took place during a Vacation Bible School (VBS) class at Sunnyland. Deanna Shoesmith was tremendous with bringing children to VBS. Her car was full and overflowing with students. I was teaching the teen class, and our lessons were about the missionary journeys of Saint Paul. One day the lesson was about Paul being stoned and being left for dead. One of the students got a rather faraway look in her eyes. I asked Kim if she had a question. She said, "Yes, what is this about Saint Paul getting drunk." Poor Kim came from a rather rough environment, and when I spoke about Saint Paul being stoned, she thought of alcoholic beverages causing him to pass out or become stoned instead of large rocks being thrown at the apostle, knocking him unconscious. It is important to make the Bible lessons understandable to the students to whom you are ministering.

We had a revival September 5-22, 1974, with Reverend George Harvey. The weather was picture perfect for that meeting. We went door to door around the church inviting people to the revival. The evangelist and I followed up on many leads inviting family and friends of the church people to the revival. One day we went to a tavern and called on Bill, the bartender. He took the invitation but trembled as we spoke to him about coming to the revival. His wife had been in the hospital, and I had called on her several times. Neither Bill nor his wife came to the revival, but I never shall forget going into the bar and how the revival announcement shook in his hand.

We called on so many people and did so much walking during that meeting that I wore a hole in one of my shoes. George Harvey was a man who sought needy souls for Christ. I remember him saying when we passed people along the street, "Potential holiness people on every corner. God can save them and sanctify them and make saints out of every one of them." It was no wonder that George started over a dozen holiness churches in his lifetime. He saw potential everywhere he looked and was an inspiration with whom to work.

God blessed the move to Sunnyland in many wonderful ways. Psalm 122:1 says, "I was glad when they said unto me, Let us go into the house of the LORD." I also like what Zechariah 8:21b says, "Let us go speedily to pray before the LORD, and to seek the LORD of hosts." It was a blessing from the Lord to have a good building in which to worship the Lord Jesus Christ.

Story 53

Revival in December

The congregation of the Peoria Wesleyan Holiness Church dearly loved Reverend Archie B. Atwell and enjoyed having him come to the church for revival meetings. He kept a full slate and was booked many years ahead. When he came for a revival in the spring of 1971, the church booked him for another meeting. The first date he had available was December 14-23, 1973. The church accepted that date and scheduled a meeting.

My wife had known Archie Atwell and his family for several years, but I was not well acquainted with him or his family. When he came, we got to know each other better and became close friends.

As you can guess, the dates selected for the meeting were not ideal. Many people were involved with holiday activities, and although the local church people attended faithfully, outsiders found other things to do. During the revival meeting we received lots of snow. Schools were closed, and one night the local McDonald's was closed, but we plowed our way through the snow and had services. It was certainly poor weather conditions for a revival. The Lord was not hindered by our obstacles and was pleased to visit the services with His presence and power. The saints were encouraged, and many were blessed in spite of the circumstances.

Archie Atwell was considering making a trip one night after service to get some eggs and frozen frying chickens from his brother in Eldon, Missouri. It had stopped snowing, but conditions were not ideal to make a trip of 340 miles each direction between services in a revival. He asked me to go with him, and I consented. After the service on Friday night, December 21, we left. We had traveled only about an hour when Archie asked me to drive his Dodge Dart. I got behind the wheel near Springfield, Illinois, and soon we hit slick roads. I passed a semi stopped in the slow lane of I-55, and the driver was putting chains on his big rig. I drove about 40 miles per hour all the way to St. Louis.

When we got on I-70, the roads were much better, and Archie agreed to drive again. I readily consented to let him have the wheel. He drove to his mother's home, arriving about 5:45 a.m. We took a short nap, and I awoke to the smell of bacon frying. She prepared a country breakfast of eggs, bacon, biscuits and gravy with home-canned jam. It was delicious.

Soon after breakfast we got the frozen chickens and a 30-dozen case of eggs. In order to carry such a large load, he strapped several boxes of chicken to the roof of the car and put the eggs in the trunk. I think there were over three hundred pounds of frozen chicken plus the eggs. His brother figured up the bill and then wrote, "Paid in full—Merry Christmas, Archie!"

In a short time we were on our way back to Peoria. The road conditions were much better, especially with the sun melting the ice. We arrived back at the parsonage in time to shave off two-days growth of whiskers and get ready to go to Francis and Melba Lee's home for the evening meal. Needless to say we were rather weary as we entered the sanctuary that night, but the Holy Spirit was pleased to come in a powerful way. Many people testified and praised the Lord, others sought the Lord, and the evangelist did not preach.

It was a very cold Saturday night, so Archie parked his Dodge Dart in our garage. He left for Michigan after the service on Sunday night and did not lose any of his frozen fryers or one of his many eggs.

There were many things about that revival that were less than perfect: a large snowfall, very cold temperatures, and the Christmas holiday activities, but God blessed that meeting. No one that attended ever forgot the revival just before Christmas in 1973.

The Bible says in Isaiah 55:10-11: "For as the rain cometh down, and the snow from heaven, and returneth not thither, but watereth the earth, and maketh it bring forth and bud, that it may give seed to the sower, and bread to the eater: So shall my word be that goeth forth out of my mouth: it shall not return unto me void, but it shall accomplish that which I please, and it shall prosper in the thing whereto I sent it."

For many years on the Manley farm, we planted red clover seed with a horn seeder while we walked through the fields in February, broadcasting the tiny red clover seeds. Sometimes we sowed the seeds when there was snow on the ground. Even the seeds planted in the snow produced a harvest. The revival with Archie Atwell was certainly a time of sowing gospel seeds in the snow.

Story 54

Wintertime in Illinois

The weather was very cold in the Peoria area during our four winters there. It was common for the temperature to drop to twenty degrees below zero. Snow was frequent as well, and sometimes we received a great amount of it.

One Wednesday night when we went to prayer meeting, there was snow on the ground, and the temperature was close to zero. That night I spoke about temptation and emphasized that everyone is tempted, the saved and the unsaved. The problem comes when one yields to temptation. The service closed, and the people were leaving the church. My wife, daughter, and I got into the Plymouth, but when I turned the key, nothing happened. The only family left at the church was the Shoesmiths, and they were about to leave. I quickly got out of the car and stopped them. I thought the battery needed a jump, but when I raised the hood, I discovered my nearly new battery was missing. The Shoesmiths helped us that night, and the next day I bought a new battery. I placed a chain and lock around it because the hood did not lock from the inside.

I was the district youth leader on the North Central District, and we planned for a New Year's rally at Springfield, Illinois. My wife, Brenda, and I had been visiting my parents and were planning to travel to Springfield from the farm. We awoke on January 1, 1974, to sub-zero weather. I tried to start the Plymouth, but it flooded. We tried everything to get that car started. Leta Henthorn, our neighbor, even pulled it with her truck, and it still would not start. We had to remove the spark plugs, dry them, and get out the excess gas. It finally started, and we made it to the youth rally on time but what a challenge that cold weather caused us.

In the 1970s, snow tires often were mounted on an extra set of wheels, and one was used for a spare and the other stored during the summer months. Then in November or early December, the snow tires were put on the rear of the car. One tire with regular tread was used as a spare, and the other tire was placed in storage.

My old snow tires were badly worn in 1974, and the one in storage was flat. I was short on money and could not afford new snow tires. I got a screwdriver-type device to plug the two holes in the tire, and on December 2, I put them on the Plymouth. It was the best I could do with winter approaching

I received a phone call on Wednesday, December 11, from Jack Hysel, the local Bible Methodist pastor in Peoria, asking me to come by the church after prayer meeting that night. That was a rather strange request, but my wife, children, and I complied. He said, "I heard you were having a rough time, and our church wanted to give you something to help." He handed me a check for $125.00. We were overjoyed. That very week I purchased two new snow tires for $64.54 and had some extra money to spend for Christmas. Praise the Lord!

We found that God met our many needs every season of the year as the Bible says in Psalm 74:17, "Thou hast set all the borders of the earth: thou hast made summer and winter." Regardless of the time or the season, God provided for us, and we thanked Him for His bountiful supply.

Story 55

Revival at All Tribes Indian Mission School

Our church was interested in spreading the gospel and had representatives from All Tribes Indian Mission School near Bernalillo, New Mexico, visit the church. Lester Wiseman was the superintendent, and he and his family stopped by our home and represented the Indian school at the church. My wife and I became good friends with the Wiseman family.

Lester invited me to come for a school revival for January 23-February 3, 1974. I was overjoyed with the invitation and previously had never visited the state of New Mexico. The gasoline crunch was a problem at that time. My wife was eight months pregnant and would need the Plymouth while I was away. I learned that I could take Amtrak from Chillicothe, Illinois, to Albuquerque, New Mexico, for $90.00 round-trip by using the clergy fare, so I opted to go by train.

I left Chillicothe on January 22 at 9:40 p.m. We made stops along the way and took on passengers; some stops were in Kansas. In the early morning darkness, we took on a rather noteworthy passenger. A very large man seated himself a couple seats in front of me along the aisle. Soon we were moving again, and the swaying cars put us to sleep along with the new passenger who snored up a storm. He enjoyed his rest; however, those around him could not sleep because of his loud snoring.

We traveled from Kansas through Colorado and entered New Mexico near Raton. The trip through the mountains was very lovely. I could envision covered wagons pulled by mules and horses coming through those rocky passes. At last the train pulled up at the Albuquerque train station. I got my luggage and disembarked, still swaying after being on board for twenty-one hours. Lester's smiling face greeted me at the train station at 5:40 p.m. local time. I was in the chapel by 7:30 for the first service of the revival. I must admit I had to hold onto the pulpit that night as I continued swaying from my long train ride from Illinois to New Mexico.

It was a highlight of my ministry to preach to the precious Native American children and pray with them as they sought Jesus at the altar. Sometimes as I walked to the chapel, the students in the dormitories would call out to me, "Hello, preacher." It was a blessing to my soul to share the Word of God with those dear children and staff members.

One day Larry Salway, a staff member, took me to the top of the Sandia Mountain. It was an awesome sight to view the splendor of that high peak.

During the revival I was made aware of the many needs of operating a boarding school with several students and staff members and their children. While I was praying about the needs of the school one day, I was reminded of my farmer father who recently had two Black Angus calves stray from his farm. I thought about the passage in I Samuel 6:10-12: "And the men did so; and took two milch kine, and tied them to the cart, and shut up their calves at home: And they laid the ark of the LORD upon the cart, and the coffer with the mice of gold and the images of their emerods. And the kine took the straight way to the way of Bethshemesh, and went along the highway, lowing as they went, and turned not aside to the right hand or to the left; and the lords of the Philistines went after them unto the border of Bethshemesh."

As a farm boy from Fishhook, I knew that milk cows never would leave their calves behind and pull a cart in the opposite direction unless God was directing them. I continued to pray about the needs of the school and felt impressed of the Lord to pray for my father's two lost calves to return home, thinking that if the Lord would send them back to the Manley farm, perhaps my father would sell one and give the money to the All Tribes Indian Mission School. I prayed and wrote my father about my impression.

Soon a Black Angus calf appeared on the Manley farm. Dad said it was not one of those that had left but was a different one. My parents contacted surrounding farmers to see if it was their calf. Several came and looked at the calf, but no one claimed it. Mom ran an ad in the paper but still no one claimed the calf. In due time Dad sold the calf and sent the money to All Tribes Indian Mission School, and Lester Wiseman bought a cow and butchered it for the kitchen. Dad never got his two calves back, but he got a blessing out of that strange prayer of his oldest son and was glad to have a part in helping the school.

On Saturday, February 2, Lester with his son, David, and I traveled to the mission station known as Rincon Marquez. It was my first visit to a Navajo Indian reservation. We spent time with the missionaries and then visited a hogan. A hogan is the traditional round earth-covered house of the Navajo Indian people. My heart was touched by the poverty of the Native American people. The spiritual needs were even more overwhelming than the poverty.

Sunday was the last day of the revival, and the Lord gave us a wonderful closing out with several seeking the Lord at the altar of prayer. On Monday at 1:20 p.m., I got back on the Amtrak train and swayed my way eastward for twenty-one long hours. I arrived in Chillicothe at 11:20 the following day, happy to be home with my darling wife and Brenda.

That revival was my first cross-culture experience with sharing the gospel. It made a lasting mark upon my life. I have never been the same. Jesus said in Mark 16:15-16: "Go ye into all the world, and preach the gospel to every creature. He that believeth and is baptized shall be saved; but he that believeth not shall be damned."

Story 56

The Birth of Our Son

It was spitting snow the morning of February 25, 1974, when my wife and I left our nineteen-month-old daughter, Brenda, with Melba Lee, and we headed for the Methodist Hospital. Again, my wife did not spend much time alone in the hospital. Soon John Russell was born at 9:21 a.m. He weighed 8 pounds and 10 ounces and was 20½ inches long.

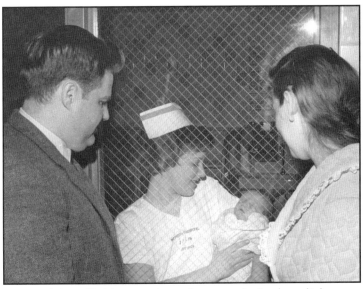
John with his parents and a nurse in the hospital

I was in the fathers' waiting room, called by some the fathers' sweatbox, when I was asked who our family pediatrician was. I was told that our son had been given some of mommy's medicine. My wife later learned that a student nurse accidentally gave baby John his mother's vitamin-K shot, and he became very active. John was placed under observation in isolation. At that time we were unaware of the gravity of the situation. Looking back, we realize that but for the mercy of God, the day of John's birth could have been the day of his death.

The Lord answered prayer; John recovered and was a normal baby boy. John Manley has been a family name for many generations. My great-grandfather was John Wesley Manley. My grandfather was Cale John Manley. My dad was skipped as he is Harry Russell Manley. I am John Stevan Manley. My son is John Russell

Baby John with his mother and sister Brenda

Manley. His son is Camden John Manley. Do you get the idea that we like the name John Manley?

We did not have insurance when John was born. Each time Helen went for a doctor's appointment, she paid toward the doctor's fees. God graciously supplied the needs for the hospital bill. The hospital gave ordained ministers a 25 percent discount, and with that discount the total bill was $374.97. The Lord laid it upon the hearts of two individuals to give us a total of $350.00 toward the

Four generations of Manleys: Cale John, Harry Russell, me, John Russell

expenses. Somehow we scraped together the $24.97 and paid the bill when we received it. Praise God for needs supplied!

Looking back over those years of our first pastorate, we saw the hand of the Lord upon our lives time and time again. We learned many valuable lessons of faith and trusting God to meet needs which helped us over the course of life. It was thrilling to watch Him move in marvelous ways His wonders to perform.

The Bible says in Jeremiah 1:5 and 7b: "Before I formed thee in the belly I knew thee; and before thou camest forth out of the womb I sanctified thee, and I ordained thee a prophet unto the nations. For thou shalt go to all that I shall send thee, and whatsoever I command thee thou shalt speak."

On February 25, 2012, my wife and I were with our son John and his family and celebrated his thirty-eighth birthday. The following day I preached at the Wesleyan Evangelistic Church in Dayton, Ohio, where he was serving as pastor. I was reminded that God had plans for a baby boy who was given the wrong medication on the day of his birth and spared his life to preach the gospel and serve the Lord Jesus Christ as His servant. Thank God for His mercy and grace.

The Steve Manley family in 1974

Story 57

God Blessed Those Washing Machines

Our years in Peoria were years of watching the Lord supply our needs and answering prayer in many wonderful ways. The friendship between Reverend and Mrs. C. Dean Grant and our family grew during our first pastorate. They also were accustomed to seeing God bless and work in matters small and large. He frequently would say, "To get a deal is not good enough. We need a deal on a deal." Many were the times when we saw the Lord stretch dollars, bless things beyond their normal life expectancy, and prove Himself to be faithful to His children.

Soon after we moved to East Peoria, Francis Lee got an old wringer washing machine from work and gave it to us. The wringer would not lock, so I cut a 2 x 4 and placed it under the handle to squeeze the water from the clothes. Then Oliver Hamilton gave us a better wringer washing machine that Dean Grant repaired. The third wringer washing machine that was given to us was from my wife's sister Joan. It was a very nice Maytag that we brought back from Michigan to Illinois. We removed the back seat of the Plymouth and placed the washer inside our vehicle to transport it.

For several years my dear wife had used wringer washing machines to do our laundry. We now had two babies in cloth diapers that you recycled by washing. I know you have to be very old to remember cloth diapers, but our babies wore them. Dean felt that we were long overdue for replacing the wringer washer with an automatic model. One day while going to garage sales, Wilma, his wife, found a copper colored Speed Queen washing machine for only $10.00. The machine outwardly looked good, but it had water inside because something was wrong, and it would not spin out the water.

Wilma thought her husband could fix it, and we could have that long-overdue automatic washer. Dean and I went to the garage sale and looked at the machine. The owner came down to $5.00, and on August 2, 1974, we became the proud owners of a Speed Queen automatic washing machine. We brought it home in the trunk of our Plymouth. Dean took the timer apart and filed the points, and it worked as good as new. We had it for seven years, and it still was operating when we purchased a new washing machine at Montgomery Wards.

The Bible says in Proverbs 10:22, "The blessing of the LORD, it maketh rich, and he addeth no sorrow with it." The blessing of the Lord was upon that Speed Queen for hundreds of loads of laundry.

God has blessed many things for the Manley family like automobiles, washing machines, vacuum cleaners, and a dozen and one other things. To God be all the glory for His manifold blessings to us.

Story 58

Driving a School Bus Again

The congregation failed to grow as rapidly as my family. In fact, we faced a decline, and I began to look at yellow school buses as a way of increasing our family income. I applied for employment at the East Peoria Community High School as a bus driver.

Don Carroll was superintendent of transportation. I liked Don from the first time I met him. I was hired and prepared to get my chauffeur's license. Because I had driven buses in Kansas, it was no big deal to drive a bus in Illinois. A driver went with me to the license bureau for the driving test. The bus that we took that day had a different shifting pattern than the one with which I had trained. On that bus third gear was where second gear was on the training bus. Being rather nervous, I put it in third gear instead of second gear to cross the railroad tracks and failed the test. It was not easy to go back to the bus garage and report that I failed the test and had to take it again. Humble pie may be good for you, but it surely tastes bad. However, I passed the test the next time I went.

On October 22, 1974, I again was driving a school bus. Frankly, I enjoyed shifting the gears and working with the students. For the most part I had good students and problems were few. I started part-time and drove the opposite shifts of a fireman who was also a bus driver. One day a student lit a firecracker on the bus as we drove up the hill to Creve Coeur. It was a foolish thing to do and caused some students to lose their hearing temporarily.

Another time a student got upset at me about a corrective measure I had taken. When he got off the bus, he made a snowball with a rock in it and threw it at me after the last student got off the bus. Thankfully, the rock-packed snowball missed me, but it put a crack in the window that it hit.

One day while I was driving, I overheard the female students directly behind me talking about religion and the Bible. One young lady said, "I know a verse in the Bible. It is John 3:16, 'For God so loved the world, that he gave his only begotten Son, that whosoever believeth in him should not perish, but have everlasting life.'" I thought to myself, *She quoted it perfectly*. Then she said something that made my heart sink. "I can quote it, but I do not know what it means." Sad to say she is not alone. Many people know verses in the Bible, but they do not know what they mean or how to apply them to their lives.

Romans 10:14-15 says: "How then shall they call on him in whom they have not believed? and how shall they believe in him of whom they have not heard? and how shall they hear without a preacher? And how shall they preach, except they be sent? as it is written, How beautiful are the feet of them that preach the gospel of peace, and bring glad tidings of good things!" Believers have an awesome responsibility of helping people to understand the Word of God.

Story 59

Two Odd Things

People sometimes say things to the minister that are rather pointed after he leads the service and preaches his sermon. On one such occasion during the opening exercise of a service, I mentioned that some people are like the friends of the little red hen. They are not willing to work for the Lord or to help around the church, but they want to receive all the blessings that are outpoured. Like the friends of the little red hen who were not willing to help prepare the bread, they want to eat the bread after it has been prepared by someone else.

On the way out of church, a certain person made it very clear that I should go home and read I Peter 4:11. I asked if that referred to using fables, and the individual assured me that it did. I am not sure if I heard wrong or if the person gave the wrong Bible reference, but I went home and turned to I Peter 4:11-13 and read these words: "If any man speak, let him speak as the oracles of God; if any man minister, let him do it as of the ability which God giveth: that God in all things may be glorified through Jesus Christ, to whom be praise and dominion for ever and ever. Amen. Beloved, think it not strange concerning the fiery trial which is to try you, as though some strange thing happened unto you: But rejoice, inasmuch as ye are partakers of Christ's sufferings; that, when his glory shall be revealed, ye may be glad also with exceeding joy." That passage was indeed a blessing to my soul. I think the desired reference was I Timothy 4:7, "But refuse profane and old wives' fables, and exercise thyself rather unto godliness." I learned a valuable lesson that day from the little red hen and two passages of Scripture.

******

After completing the requirements for my Bachelor of Arts degree in Missions, I mailed a check to KCCBS on May 5, 1975, for the required fees and tuition costs. That afternoon our old refrigerator stopped working. Why would something like that happen on the very day I had just spent money to advance my education? I do not know the why, but it was a trial. We purchased a used refrigerator and got by with it okay. However, one month and a day later, on June 6, a family gave the church a one-year-old refrigerator for the parsonage. When we left that pastorate, the church board voted to give us the refrigerator. God does work in mysterious ways His wonders to perform.

Romans 8:28 says, "And we know that all things work together for good to them that love God, to them who are the called according to his purpose." Even when odd and strange things happen to us, we know that God can and does work them together for our good. I am thankful that He has done that in my life many times.

Story 60

Time to Move

Just as the Lord directs a minister to accept a pastorate, He also directs him to move to another charge. As the spring of 1975 came to Illinois, a growing conviction came to my soul that it was time for me to resign from the church and move to another one. I had not received any invitations to pastor other churches, but I felt restless in my soul and knew I soon would be leaving as pastor of the Sunnyland Wesleyan Holiness Church.

Our annual church meeting was held on April 18, 1975. Robert Fleming was the district superintendent, and he presided over the meeting. I told him prior to the business meeting that I planned to resign at the annual meeting. He told me that I should not resign until I had a place to go. His many years in the ministry dictated that it was foolhardy for a man with a wife and two small children to resign with no place to go and no means of supporting himself. When the vote for pastor was taken, I received a unanimous recall from the faithful but small membership of the church. I had my letter ready to read after the vote. However, Superintendent Fleming did not allow me to speak but moved right on to the election of Sunday school superintendent, thus closing the door for me to resign that night.

In the kind providence of God, it was a good thing I did not resign on April 18 as I had planned because it was not until September that God opened all the doors so that we could move to our next pastorate.

I worked part-time at the bus garage with Don Carroll during the summer of 1975. The government had changed the law, and all school buses needed to be equipped with the eight-light warning system. Some of the older buses needed to be equipped with the yellow lights that were now required. I helped with that project as well as to change oil and do other maintenance work on the buses. One day I was to install a new rubber mat on the steps of one of the buses. It was a very hot summer day, and the mat refused to fit properly. I was getting nowhere with the job. All I accomplished was to get my shirt wet with perspiration. Don came over and said, "Go, get a drink of water. Sit down and rest and come back and try it again." I obeyed his suggestion and got the mat installed. That was a great lesson.

It was not easy to wait upon the Lord when I felt in my heart that I should be moving from the Peoria area and pastoring another church. That was a good time to consider II Peter 1:5-8: "And beside this, giving all diligence, add to your faith virtue; and to virtue knowledge; And to knowledge temperance; and to temperance patience; and to patience godliness; And to godliness brotherly kindness; and to brotherly kindness charity. For if these things be in you, and abound, they make you that ye shall neither be barren nor unfruitful in the knowledge of our Lord Jesus Christ."

Story 61

Tents and Tent Meetings

I have been attracted to tents for many years. When I was a small boy, our family went camping with friends along McKee Creek and spent the night in a tent. A few years later, I went by a gospel tent that was pitched at Highland school and saw people having church services at night where Ed Null was preaching. After my conversion I attended tent meetings in Curryville and Elsberry, Missouri, where Melvin Kirks was the evangelist. There was something exciting to me about having services in a tent. I also noticed that spiritually needy people tended more readily to come to services in a tent than in a church.

My brother Rodney attended one of Ed Null's tent meetings in Adams County, Illinois, and heard Ed say, "I would be willing to give this tent to someone who would use it in holiness evangelism." Something on the inside of me did a cartwheel. Wow! A tent to use to hold tent revivals and free of charge. I was interested indeed. At the time I was living in East Peoria, and Ed Null lived in Lauderdale, Mississippi.

I purchased a homemade enclosed trailer in which to store the tent, chairs, pulpit, altar, and lights. Arrangements were made for

Plymouth Fury and enclosed trailer for tent storage

Rodney and me to take my father's nearly brand-new Chevy pickup to Mississippi and get the tent right after Rodney graduated from high school. We left very early in the morning of May 31, 1973, and drove all day. We thought once we crossed into northern Mississippi, we were almost there, but that was not the case. We traveled many miles in that long state. Ed's wife served us a wonderful Southern supper soon after we arrived. We loaded the tent, poles, fifty chairs, pulpit and altar, and the lights into Dad's pickup.

Standing in front of the newly acquired tent

Ed Null then took us to the barn to see his special horse named Happy. That was no normal Tennessee Walking Horse. Ed had taught Happy to do fifty tricks. The horse could count, play dead, roll over, pull a handkerchief out of Ed's pocket, and many more tricks. Happy was truly an amazing horse. We spent the night with the Nulls and made our way back to Fishhook the next day. Rodney and I put the tent and equipment in the trailer and stored it in Dad's barn. I was a busy pastor at the time as our church had purchased a different building and was moving to Sunnyland.

The first time the tent was used was in a Wesleyan Holiness home-missions revival in Canton, Illinois, about thirty-five miles from Peoria. A vacant lot was rented, and the tent was erected on September 24, 1973. We chose to use one pole and make it circular and about forty feet in diameter, in which manner it easily could seat one hundred people; however, we only had fifty chairs so we borrowed some.

The Lord helped us, but it was a great learning experience. September is rather late for a tent meeting as the evenings get rather cool, and it gets dark before you start the service. We also soon learned that a portable toilet was as important as electric lights. Various preachers and singers were used which did not lead to continuity. The tent was taken down on October 12 and taken back to Dad's barn for storage inside the trailer.

We hoped to use the tent in a revival meeting in Davenport, Iowa, but because of many city ordinances, it was cost prohibitive. We used the Salvation Army Citadel for the revival instead of the tent.

The Great Lakes District of the Wesleyan Holiness Association of Churches needed a larger tabernacle for their July 1975 camp

Tent in use near Remus, MI. Brenda in the foreground.

160

meeting near Remus, Michigan. I agreed to let them use the tent and also consented to take it to Michigan for the camp meeting. That was my wife's home camp meeting, so we went early to pitch the tent and remained for the entire camp. That time the tent was pitched to its full size of forty feet by eighty feet. It was an awesome sight to pull onto the campgrounds and see the huge tent. It could seat 250 to 300 people. The evangelists that year were L.J. Cherryholmes and L. Wayne States. We had a great camp.

Moving to the new pastorate in Ann Arbor, MI
Brenda and John by the U-HAUL truck

At the close of the camp, I was asked to go to Ann Arbor, Michigan, and preach for the Wednesday evening prayer meeting because their pastor had resigned. It was a trial sermon so that the people there could consider me for their pastor. We enjoyed being with Matthew Harden, the newly elected assistant general superintendent. The next day we returned to our home in East Peoria and found that it had been sold, and we would need to move within 40 to 45 days. That had a way of intensifying our prayers. Soon a vote was taken at Ann Arbor, a call was extended for me to come as pastor, and I accepted. The Lord asked me if I could love the people, and I told Him I could. I resigned the Wesleyan Holiness Church in Sunnyland and moved to Ann Arbor.

Psalm 119:133 records the prayer, "Order my steps in thy word: and let not any iniquity have dominion over me." My wife and I desired that our steps would be ordered by the Lord in the move to Michigan, and we truly believed they were.

Story 62

Reflections

Looking back over the four years we lived in East Peoria, I am very thankful that the Lord led my wife and me there. The people were wonderful to a young pastor fresh out of Bible school. They treated us with love and respect. We learned several valuable lessons, made many great friends, and made more than a few mistakes in a small forgiving church. Most of the dear people we shepherded then have left this world already, and hopefully we helped them on their journey to the celestial city.

The lessons of faith in God and the joy of trusting Him to supply our needs, whether large or small, marked us for life. The Lord was gracious to us during those years of our early ministry in the Peoria metro area.

We met people during those years with whom we have crossed paths many times and, in some instances, have worked closely with them on several occasions. The evangelists that came to our church were Glenn Griffith, L. Wayne States, Larry Warren, Archie B. Atwell, Elmer Long, Mike Watson, George Harvey, Jack Dulin, Charles Denniston, and Richard Ringle. Special speakers in area churches allowed us to hear some great servants of the Lord, many for the first time, like J. Wesley Adcock, H. Robb French, L.W. Barbee, Guy Mowery, David Light, August Luelf, Winfield Poe, Noel Scott, R.E. Carroll, R.W. Eichel, V.O. Agan, Marshall Smart, H.E. Darnell, Irene Hanley, and Remos Rehfeldt

It was a privilege to serve the Lord and the people in our first pastorate. Their love and support were an encouragement to a young pastor.

God Loves You

For God so loved the world, that he gave his only begotten Son, that whosoever believeth in him should not perish, but have everlasting life. —John 3:16

But God commendeth his love toward us, in that, while we were yet sinners, Christ died for us. —Romans 5:8

All Have Sinned

For all have sinned, and come short of the glory of God. —Romans 3:23

As it is written, There is none righteous, no, not one.—Romans 3:10

God's Solution for Sin

For the wages of sin is death; but the gift of God is eternal life through Jesus Christ our Lord. —Romans 6:23

But as many as received him, to them gave he power to become the sons of God, even to them that believe on his name. —John 1:12

For I delivered unto you first of all that which I also received, how that Christ died for our sins according to the scriptures; And that he was buried, and that he rose again the third day according to the scriptures. —I Corinthians 15:3-4

You May Be Saved Now

Behold, I stand at the door, and knock: if any man hear my voice, and open the door, I will come in to him. —Revelation 3:20a

For whosoever shall call upon the name of the Lord shall be saved. —Romans 10:13

My Decision to Receive Christ as My Savior

Confessing to God that I am a sinner, and believing that the Lord Jesus Christ died for my sins on the cross and was raised for my justification, I do now renounce my sins and receive and confess Him as my personal Savior.

Name _____

Date _____

Finding a Church

After receiving Christ as your Savior, you are encouraged to prayerfully seek a local church that will assist you in your growing as a new Christian by the clear teaching of the Bible. If you need assistance you may contact Steve Manley at efmjsm@juno.com.